EAL in the Early Years

Hundreds of ideas for supporting children with English as an Additional Language

Anita Soni

FEATHERSTONE
AN IMPRINT OF BLOOMSBURY
L   DNEY

Published 2013 by Featherstone, an imprint of Bloomsbury Publishing plc
50 Bedford Square, London, WC1B 3DP
www.bloomsbury.com

ISBN 978-1-4081-5987-3

Text © Anita Soni 2013

Photographs with kind permission of:
Little Angels Schoolhouse, Hackney, London;
Acorn Childcare Ltd, Milton Keynes.

A CIP catalogue for this book is available from the British Library.

Printed and bound in India by Replika Press Pvt. Ltd

10 9 8 7 6 5 4 3 2 1

This book is produced using paper that is made from wood grown in
managed, sustainable forests. It is natural, renewable and recyclable.
The logging and manufacturing process conform to the environmental
regulations of the country of origin.

To see our full range of titles visit www.bloomsbury.com

Contents

X6708
428.4245oiN
CuC

X6708
428.4245oiN
CuC

Introduction

There is much that can be done to support the children that are learning EAL in our early years settings. This book is intended to bridge theory and practice by giving an overview of the theories of language acquisition alongside practical ideas on how best to support EAL learners. The three aims of the book are:

- That it is a tool that supports staff in reflecting on their practice;
- That it is a resource that can be used to inform staff development;
- That it is a source of practical ideas on how best to support EAL.

Issues of cultural diversity have to be considered when learning EAL. This book considers these needs alongside the guidance given within the Early Years Foundation Stage (EYFS) documentation (DfE, 2012), in order to consider how best to support children in the areas of learning and development.

Other key issues such as the characteristics of effective learning, observation, assessment and planning, the environment, the Key Person approach and Special Educational Needs will also be discussed.

The chapters of this book do not have to be read in sequence. It is intended to be practical, provide relevant background and understanding and promote reflective practice. All chapters contain key messages, and Chapters 4 to 10 contain audits and self-evaluation activities to support practitioners in reflecting upon their practice.

If you are interested in the definitions of terms such as bilingualism, multilingualism and EAL, then have a look at Chapter 1. This chapter explains the changes in approaches to EAL and some of the theories and research that underpin current understanding of best practice. It also examines how language and cognition relate to each other in terms of EAL learners.

Chapter 2 is a practical chapter that looks at how early years settings can get started in their work with EAL. It considers what to do before a child arrives at the setting and some suggested ideas for the first few days and weeks. There is also a questionnaire to help reflect on practice.

Chapter 3 examines and unpicks the requirements in the Statutory Framework for the EYFS (DfE 2012) in supporting EAL. It details the practical implications of these requirements.

In Chapter 4, the prime areas of learning and development from the EYFS – Personal, Social and Emotional Development (PSED), Communication and Language, and Physical Development – are examined to consider how best to support EAL learners. There are also activities and questions for you to reflect upon, in order that you can applaud existing good practice and seek to develop it further.

Chapter 5 is written in a similar way to Chapter 4 and deals with the specific areas of learning and development: Literacy, Mathematics, Understanding the World and Expressive Arts and Design. It uses the material provided in Development Matters in the EYFS to consider the support needed for EAL learners, alongside other supporting research and information.

Chapters 6 to 9 consider key issues within early years practice, and how these relate to supporting children learning EAL. Chapter 6 starts with observation, assessment and planning. Chapter 7 looks at the Key Person approach, and how this alongside partnership with parents can be used to effectively support EAL learners. Chapter 8 considers how the environment of the setting can be optimised to enhance the experiences of the children learning EAL. Chapter 9 examines the characteristics of effective learning from within Development Matters in the Early Years Foundation Stage, and how these can be supported with children learning EAL.

Chapter 10 explores issues surrounding identification of Special Educational Needs in children learning English as an Additional Language. It also considers how best to support children learning EAL who have Special Educational Needs (SEN).

Chapters 11 and 12 are intended to support settings in developing or enhancing their work with children learning EAL. They contain activities, case studies and questions to reflect upon, in order to evaluate how well the setting is progressing and to recognise and celebrate what is going well and develop this further.

I hope that you find this book useful for your practice. Supporting children learning English as an Additional Language is not easy, but it can be rewarding and fun! I hope this book will support you, in order to best support your children.

CHAPTER 1

What are bilingualism, EAL and multilingualism?

This chapter explores the many definitions of bilingualism and how the term has changed over time. It considers when a person can or should describe him or herself as bilingual, and the factors that influence a person's use of one language rather than another. This chapter also considers how a child acquires two languages, and the implications of the process of language acquisition.

Before you begin this chapter reflect on the following questions:

REFLECTION POINT

Do you describe yourself as monolingual or bilingual? Why is that?

Is anyone really monolingual?

What does bilingualism mean?

When the term bilingual is used, it is typically used to describe a person who can use two languages. However, whether or not people consider themselves to be bilingual varies from person to person, as does whether a person is perceived by others to be bilingual as opposed to monolingual. Think about a child who attends your early years setting and speaks a language other than English. Is the child monolingual or bilingual? It is likely that the child may understand or speak one or two words of English, even if it is the word 'television' (which tends to be the same word in all languages). Alternatively, consider the tourist going on holiday to France having memorised a few useful French phases. Is this person bilingual?

In fact, it can be argued that it is impossible to state when a person becomes bilingual, or is bilingual – many factors, such as the individual's social, cultural and linguistic experience, have to be taken into account. Indeed, people who would often be perceived to be monolingual – in that they only speak one language – could also describe themselves as bilingual. Such people change their use of words, grammar and fluency depending upon who they are talking to and the context of the conversation. One example might be a lawyer who uses legal terms within their work but would speak in a different way and with a different emphasis when at home with his or her family. Now reflect again on the initial questions.

Is there one definition of bilingualism?

The short answer to this question is that definitions of bilingualism have changed over time. For instance, early definitions of bilingualism tended to focus on the individual's ability to speak two languages, with a focus on use of grammar or fluency rather than comprehension. Hall states that:

> 'Definitions of bilingualism over the years have focused on linguistic competence…Bilingualism does not begin until the speaker has at least some knowledge and control of the grammatical structures of the second language.'

(Hall, 1952 cited by Miller, 1978)

However, in more recent years the focus on speaking skills alone has been recognised as insufficient and the importance of comprehension has been recognised. An example of this comes from Madhani. This more holistic viewpoint describes bilingual competence as:

'...understanding and using two or more languages to varying degrees and at various times.'

(Madhani, 1994 cited in Buckley, 2003).

Harding-Esch and Riley (1986) sum up the difficulties in defining bilingualism in absolute terms, stating that:

'Bilingualism is not a black-and-white, all-or-nothing phenomenon; it is more or less.'

The unique way people acquire and use language makes it difficult to define bilingualism accurately. It is a subjective and personal view.

Does bilingualism mean the person uses exactly the same amount of each language?

In reality it is unrealistic to aim for people to be absolutely equal in their use of both languages, since the use of either language depends on the individual's circumstances and the society in which they live.

One reason for a bilingual person to use one language more than another language may relate to how the languages are perceived in their society. For example, a bilingual person might live in a country that is predominantly populated by people who are monolingual, the dominant language being different to the bilingual person's 'home' language. Bilingual speakers who live in monolingual countries can find it more difficult to maintain their home language. This is because it is socially unacceptable to use their other language in public places and, as a result, bilingual speakers tend to only use their home language in their homes. This could be because monolingual speakers respond suspiciously to those who speak a different language or treat them in a negative way. So, for example, in a part of England where all the people tend to speak English alone, a person who speaks another language such as German may not use it because when they speak German, other people around them become wary and wonder what or who the person is talking about.

A second reason why a person may use one language more than another is opportunity. It is rare that a person has equal opportunities to use both languages. This tends to be influenced by the places a person goes to, the people they mix with and their life experiences in general. A person can find that one language becomes more dominant simply because it is used more frequently.

A third reason that a person may speak more of one language than another is about the two languages spoken. There are some languages that are viewed as more socially acceptable than others.

REFLECTION POINT

Think about how the following languages are valued in schools? Which order would you put these languages in?

French, Spanish, German, Punjabi, Somali, Russian and Arabic

Hall (1995) categorises different groups of bilingual children as described in the table below:

Elite bilinguals	Children of families who travel to other countries for choice; either for business, academic or diplomatic reasons. The first language of the children is not threatened and is maintained in the home and through regular visits to their home country. For these children bilingualism is seen as enriching and they are unlikely to experience subtractive bilingualism.
Linguistic majorities	Children are within a large group where they are learning a second language as this is a more prestigious language, or to learn a language quickly.
Bilingual families	Children come from families where one parent speaks a different language to the dominant language of the country. There is no pressure beyond those of the family or culture to learn the language.
Linguistic minorities	Children who come from families where the status and value of the language is low in the country. Children in these families will be under pressure to learn the dominant language of the country, as there is economic pressure to be able to speak and be literate in this language. Some of the children may be part of families who are keen to maintain their home language alongside the dominant language for cultural and religious reasons.

REFLECTION POINT

Think about the following situations and decide which category each child might fit into:

1 A Pakistani child who speaks Mirpuri at home with his family, and is living in England.
2 A child who lives in France and has one parent who speaks German.
3 An English-speaking child attending immersion classes in French, with all of his friends in a French-speaking part of Canada.
4 A Spanish-speaking child who is living in Italy with her family, as her father is working there on a one-year contract.
5 A Chinese child whose family decides he should attend an English-speaking school in Hong Kong.

Where do bilingual people live?

If the world is taken as a whole, it is interesting to note that bilingualism is actually widespread in all countries except in the US and UK. Baker (1996) estimates '...two thirds of the world's population speaks more than one language.'

However, if countries are examined individually, bilingualism is localised and not as common. Whilst there are parts of both the US and the UK where there are higher numbers of people who are bilingual, this is limited to smaller, urban areas. For example, there are over 300 languages spoken in London and Birmingham; however, this does not represent the rest of England, which has high numbers of people who speak English alone.

In the US there are areas where the most common first language is not English–American, but is another language such as Spanish. The local society in which these people live maintains this situation as there is no need to acquire the majority language, in this case English, for the people to function successfully. There are comparable areas in Birmingham where there are densely populated areas where children may not need to speak English. This is because their main sources of communication are other people who speak the same language as them. The children speak to their parents and siblings in their own language, can access doctors who speak the same language, have neighbours who speak their language and there is even television broadcast in their language.

What are the patterns of bilingualism?

Children in early years settings grow up in different circumstances, and these circumstances affect the way they acquire and understand a second language, in this case English. The most common patterns of language within families who are raised bilingually from birth have been identified by Langdon and Cheng (1992) and are shown in the table below.

Language pattern	Explanation	Examples
One person – one language	This is where one adult in the family speaks one language and the other speaks another.	With a child speaking Hebrew and English, the mother speaks only Hebrew, the father speaks only English to their child. With a child speaking French and Spanish, the mother speaks French and the stepfather speaks Spanish.
One place – one language	This is where there are places where one language is spoken and other places where the other is spoken.	With a child speaking Punjabi and English, Punjabi is spoken with grandparents in their house and at the temple, and English is spoken at home and in nursery.
One time of day – one language	This is where one language is used at one time of day, and the other language is used at another time of day.	With a child speaking Chinese and English, both parents speak English during the day, and speak Chinese in the evening. Both parents have to be competent in both Chinese and English.
Alternating use of languages	This is where there are differing circumstances and places where the two languages are used.	Both parents switch between using both languages depending on contextual factors such as the other people present, the topic, the location and the activity. Both parents have to be competent in both languages.

Source: Based on patterns in language use by Langdon and Cheng, 1992 cited in Buckley, 2003, p.155

REFLECTION POINT

Do you know what languages the other children learning EAL speak?

Who they speak the different languages with?

Do you know when and where they speak each language?

See, for example, the language maps in Chapter 2 on page 14 which are a way of recording the different languages children use and understand.

How do children learn a second language?

There are two ways that children learn another language:

1   For some children, the two languages are introduced at the same time. This is known as simultaneous acquisition of two languages.

2   For some children, another language is introduced after the child has a sound command of the first language. This is known as sequential acquisition.

How does simultaneous acquisition of two languages happen?

This is when the baby experiences both languages within the family from the time it was born. The experience of when the two languages are used with the child can be different. The baby could experience any of the language patterns listed in the table on the previous page. The baby could experience one language with one person and one language with another. Equally the baby could experience different languages in different places or at different times, or a mixture of these experiences. The implication of simultaneous acquisition of two languages is that the baby experiences a wider range of sounds and learns different patterns and rules of languages. This can be very different depending on the languages spoken.

CASE STUDY

Jessie is ten months old. She hears her mum speaking in Portuguese and her dad speaking in English. Jessie recognises and enjoys the Portuguese nursery rhymes her mum sings. Even though she spends more time with her mum, she can follow simple instructions such as 'Come here', 'Stop', 'Milk' in Portuguese and English.

What is sequential acquisition of two languages?

In early years settings it is more common to encounter babies and children who have already learned their first or home language to their expected age and stage and possibly beyond, who are then learning, or have learnt, a second language such as English, after that. This is known as sequential acquisition.

If a child has not already attended an early years setting, they are more likely to experience the second language when playing with siblings and other children, when watching television or when out in the community, for example when shopping with their parents. By this point the children may already know how to communicate, why communication is important and the rules of social interaction. They may also know how language works, although this is not in technical terms such as words, grammar and phrases. Children may know:

'...that words refer to objects and events, that words can be combined to form phrases and sentences, and that application of grammatical rules can change the tense of an utterance – combined with their knowledge about communication provides children with strategies to apply when learning an additional language,'

(Madhani, 1994 cited in Buckley, 2003, p.163)

If the child is not encouraged to continue to develop their first language then there is a danger that this can lead to 'subtractive bilingualism.' This means that English becomes the child's predominant language, and in some cases children can lose the ability to communicate in their home or first language. It is important to balance a child's need to learn English with their right to maintain their first or home language.

What are the implications of simultaneous or sequential acquisition of two languages? Which is best?

In the past it has been argued that a child who experiences two or more languages from birth will be confused and that this in turn will affect their ability to communicate in later life. It can be argued that this view is still evident within English culture. This may be one of the reasons for the England being one of the few monolingual nations.

However, research in the last 20 years has offered the different viewpoint that babies can understand and differentiate between two languages:

'[...] babies appear to be biologically prepared and ready not only to acquire or learn two or more languages but also to remember and store these languages. To do this they have to be able to see the differences between these languages and to discriminate between them.'

(Meisel, 2004 and Genese, 2003, cited in Smidt, 2008, p.53)

Mehler et al. added that babies 'will babble in their stronger language and will show some language-specific babbling features in each of their languages' (Mehler et al., 1988 cited in Smidt, 2008 p.54). The research from Deuchar and Quay shows that even the youngest bilingual children are 'able to choose which language to use with which person but also to match the language to the context' (Deuchar and Quay, 2001, cited in Smidt, 2008, p.54).

This demonstrates that babies and young children have some understanding of their own language patterns. This is an aspect of their development that practitioners can overlook.

However, it is also important to recognise that babies and children will explore and experiment with both languages in different contexts and with different people. An example of this is when a new child is settling in to an early years setting and may have spoken Polish, the language he speaks at home, to his Key Person. This may be for a number of reasons, such as the child believes that all females speak Polish or that English is used only in contexts outside of the home such as in shops. Most important is to recognise that the child will experience confusion when his/her Key Person does not respond.

Sometimes when bilingual people are talking together they will use English utterances within the other language they are using. This can be for a number of different reasons such as tiredness, being distracted, not being able to think of the word in their home language. This interchangeable use of words, phases or sentences of different languages is more commonly known as code or language switching. There is no evidence to suggest that sequential bilingual learners are any less competent than simultaneous bilingual learners.

Is bilingualism beneficial to the child?

Research does suggest that bilingualism has a beneficial impact on children's academic and intellectual development which continues into adulthood. The Primary National Strategy, 2007 reminds practitioners in their guidance for supporting children learning English as an Additional Language that:

'It is widely accepted that bilingualism confers intellectual advantages and the role of the first language in the child's learning is of great importance...Home language skills are transferable to new languages and strengthen children's understanding of language use. Developing and maintaining a home language as the foundation for knowledge about language will support the development of English and should be encouraged.'

(Primary National Strategy, 2007, p.4)

Bilingualism can strengthen the understanding of language, and ultimately helps individuals to learn a third language more easily. In addition, people who are bilingual are more easily able to access more than one culture and as an adult are able to use their languages within the work environment, for example, to sell products to other countries, teach modern foreign languages or work in other countries.

However, it is more likely that children who have learnt English sequentially are below their monolingual peers when assessed at the end of the Reception year. This is because it can take up to two to three years to be fluent in a new language, and more than five years to use the cognitive and academic aspects of the language effectively.

'Although many children from EAL backgrounds who have poor outcomes at the end of the Foundation Stage go on to become the highest achieving children, there are also many who do not catch up'.

(Primary National Strategy, 2007, p.2)

Possible reasons for this include not attending an early years setting prior to their statutory school age, either through choice or due to lack of appropriate advice. It could also because of the education background of the parents, especially the mother, or any special education needs that may hinder language acquisition. This will be explained further in Chapter 10.

Is bilingualism beneficial to the setting?

In a setting where bilingualism is talked about and encouraged, all children will benefit as it improves language awareness and knowledge, promotes cultural diversity and acceptance and strengthens the children's understanding of the community in which they live.

What is 'home language'/'mother tongue'/'first language'? What is 'preferred language'? Are these all the same or are they different?

These are terms that can be used interchangeably, and may vary within textbooks and guidance. The terms tend to mean the language or languages that the child can speak or understand other than English and use within their home. This book will use the term 'home language'.

What are the learning needs of children?

Research in the 1950s suggested that the impact of learning an additional language was detrimental to a child's overall development. However, after the 1960s it was established that this was only the case for a child learning an additional language sequentially, who had not developed their first language to an adequate level of competency and as a result lost the ability to use it effectively. This was known as 'subtractive bilingualism.'

Since then, the key principle in supporting children learning EAL *is that the first language should be maintained and developed, as it has been – and still is – very significant in the child's learning and development.* This is reinforced as part of the Learning and Development Requirements of the EYFS (DfE 2012), and is discussed further in Chapter 3.

It is important that a child learning EAL continues to be cognitively challenged, in order to ensure that they can access all the learning opportunities that they need to achieve their full potential. If, from a desire to ensure that English is acquired more rapidly, a child's first language is not encouraged at home and/or in a setting this can lead to a delay in other areas of a child's development. It is important to remember that, in most cases:

'Children learning English are as able as any other children, and the learning experiences planned for them should be no less challenging'

(Primary National Strategy, 2007, p.5).

Ideally, a new concept would be introduced to a child using their first language. For example, a Hindi-speaking child would be taught or encouraged to explore 'long' and 'short' items whilst talking in Hindi. Once the child demonstrates understanding and competence, the English words for 'long' and 'short' would be introduced. The new concept of 'long and short' is more likely to be understood this way, rather than the more widespread approach of teaching the concept through English alone, a language the child is not yet fully competent in.

This is much easier in settings where a child shares the same home language as a practitioner. In these instances it is easier to establish the child's understanding and level of conceptual development, and initially teach, play and explore in the shared language. Once the concept is gained, then English words and phrases are used with the child.

A greater challenge is presented if there is no one who can speak the same language as the child. An alternative is to work closely with the parents in order to teach the child identified concepts, before or whilst they are taught in the setting, and then reinforce these concepts in English in the setting. A third solution is to identify some key words relating to the concept in the child's first or home language, and to use these in the initial stages of teaching, play and exploration, before using English later. This will also ensure the first language is maintained and the child's positive self-esteem is preserved.

What to do first when working with a child learning EAL

This chapter looks at ways of helping children, families and practitioners make a good start when working together in a new early years setting. It takes a staged response to thinking about what is needed and how to develop the practice and setting.

- Stage 1: First contact with the family – before the child arrives
- Stage 2: The family visit the setting or a home visit – before the child arrives
- Stage 3: The child arrives at the setting

At the end of this chapter is a tool to support reflection on practice in relation to transitions into the setting of children learning EAL.

When any child starts in a new setting, even a child whose first language is English, it can be an overwhelming experience. Imagine, therefore, what it feels like for a child who has little experience of the 'majority language', in this case English. This experience can be related to our own experiences as adults, either on holidays in less familiar countries or in a new work or education context, where there are new sounds, smells and visual experiences to understand. How is this done? We tend to try and understand the new experience by comparing it to one that is familiar.

First of all, it is important to remember all of the things that are done for all children who start in a new early years setting. Every setting should have a number of procedures in place to help each child and their family settle into the setting. These should also be used with children learning EAL.

Settling into a new setting can be also be a positive experience for children learning EAL, but only if practitioners plan for an effective transition. This has to be relevant for the individual child starting at the setting, and therefore should build on what the child already knows and their life experience thus far. This can be more of a challenge when trying to find out about a child and family who speak a different language and are learning EAL.

Smidt (2008) gives an analogy for a child's introduction to a new setting. In her analogy, the child is seen to be thrown in a swimming pool without any floatation aids such as arm bands and is left 'to sink or swim.' This example highlights the child's role in settling in, but overlooks the many things a practitioner can do to help the child swim and not sink. This acts as a helpful reminder of the vital role of the practitioner. Effective transition policies and procedures, alongside an inclusive environment, can provide the 'armbands' to successfully support a family and child in settling into the new setting, despite the presence of an unfamiliar culture and language.

REFLECTION POINT

Can you think of any other 'flotation devices' that you have in your setting that would help settle children learning EAL into your setting?

It is important that the setting undertakes some specific planning for a child learning EAL from the moment the family decides that their child will attend. This includes finding out about:

- the child
- the child's family
- the child's background
- the languages the child speaks at home.

This is easiest to do when family first make contact or the first time they come to look at the setting. This allows some time for the setting to find out more about the child's background and languages before s/he starts.

Stage 1: The first contact with the family – before the child arrives

The starting point for all early years settings is to ensure that they demonstrate a willing need to work in partnership with all parents and families regardless of their background, culture or languages spoken. The EYFS) (DfE 2012) identifies that the EYFS (DfE 2012, p.2) states that settings need to provide: 'partnership working between practitioners and with parents and/ or carers; and equality of opportunity and anti-discriminatory practice, ensuring that every child is included and supported. This is done by providing an environment where the family is respected, included and valued and can be created by the displays shown on the walls, the languages shown and how the staff react and respond to the child in the setting.

Therefore, it is important for practitioners to remain open minded, non-judgemental and to avoid making any assumptions or judgements. Examples of such assumptions are:

- that the parents can read and write their language as well as speak it;
- their religious beliefs are the same as the majority of people who live in that country.

These assumptions happen quickly as practitioners, like all people, are trying to make sense of what is new. However it is important to pause, reflect and check, rather than assume!

CASE STUDY

The manager at Denholm Nursery has had a phone call from a family to confirm that their child will be starting in two weeks time. The manager at the nursery offers the family either a home visit or, if the family prefers, a visit to the nursery. The family chooses a home visit. During the telephone call, the manager fills out the relevant paperwork and asks some preliminary questions about family background. These include:

- the child's (or family's) country of origin;
- how long the child has been in the country;
- the languages spoken at home.

This information will then be fed back to the child's intended Key Person who will conduct the home visit. The manager asks the parents whether they would find it helpful to have someone who can translate for some or all of the time and if a family member could do this or if they would like the nursery to provide a translator (if someone is available).

Using this information, the Key Person has looks up some relevant websites that give information on the country of origin – in this case Poland – and the language the new child speaks (Polish). The next step is to review the learning environment of Denholm Nursery using the proforma below as a guide.

	Reception Area	Learning Environment
Photographs from adults and children from different backgrounds		
Scripts from different languages including script from the new family		
Resources including books, dolls, role play resources that represent the new family		
Prompts to help the child be independent without communicating e.g. choice cards, photos of the toilet routine, peg with child's photograph on		

In consultation with the manager a number of quick adaptations are identified to be undertaken in the short term. These include:

- adding the Polish script for 'Welcome' to the Welcome sign in the Reception area
- borrow Polish dual language books from the local library;
- the Key Person prepares some additional questions about relevant cultural resources, such as books about Poland, and finding out about any possible variations in dialect.

REFLECTION POINT

Think about this case study, are there things you can see that were helpful to welcome the child and family? How could this practice be improved further?

Although all of this practice may not be possible at your setting, there may be some adaptations that you can make to improve how you start new children learning EAL.

Stage 2: The family visit the setting or a home visit – before the child arrives

The next stage in the induction process is to acquire more detailed information on the family and verify the accuracy of the research completed by the Key Person – this is important as every child and family are unique! In addition to the initial information captured on the child and family record form (see below), it is essential to ask more questions about the languages spoken, who uses them, which language the child mainly uses (example language map forms are shown on the following page) and any key words that would be helpful in supporting communication with the child.

The safeguarding and welfare requirements in the EYFS(DfE 2012) identify specific information that providers must record on each child in their care. These minimum requirements are shown in bold on the sample child and family form below. Additional information has been added which will support the smooth transition of children learning EAL into the setting. This example record can be adapted for use by the setting.

Example child and family record form

Full name	
Name child is normally called at home	
Name to be used in early years setting (ensure correct pronunciation)	
Date of birth	
Length of time in the country	
Name of those who have parental responsibility	
Address where child normally lives	
Addresses where those who have parental responsibility live	
Emergency contact details	
Previous settings attended	
Current settings child attends (shared care provision)	
Who lives in the child's house?	
Other important people in the child's life	
Details of family religion	
Festivals observed	
Toys or activities that the child likes	
How the child likes to be comforted or settled and any comfort items needed	
Medical requirements and allergies/Special Educational Needs/disabilities	
Professionals involved?	
Dietary requirements	
Skin and hair care requirements	
Any other cultural issues regarding eating, toileting etc.?	
How would the family like information to be shared e.g. email, through a friend, written diary	

Language maps

Language maps are helpful to identify the different languages a child may use or hear in their lives. It can help show the many different languages children know, and the one they hear or use the most. The first language map is based on the different people the child spends time with, the second focuses on places the child goes to. Either or both approaches can be used. These language maps are simple and can be adapted to be used by settings.

Language map showing language spoken by different people in child's life

	Mother	Father	Grand-parents	Siblings	Other relatives	Other people
Name						
Language spoken by person						
Languages written by person						
Time spent by child with person						
If person speaks more than one language, when is each spoken?						

Language map showing languages spoken in different places in child's life

	Home	Early Years setting	Doctors/ health services	Religious buildings	Other
Language spoken here					
Languages written here					
Amount of time spent here					

It is also important to understand what the parents think about the child's ability to communicate at home. Ask questions about whether the child can follow the parent's instructions in order to carry out simple tasks such as getting their coat (with or without holding the coat or pointing), whether they know the names of objects and animals and how well they play with other children. The detail of these questions will depend upon the age and stage of the child who is being discussed. If the induction meeting takes place in the family's home, the practitioners will be able to observe some of these aspects as well as observe what items could be added to the nursery's learning environment, in order to make it more familiar for the child. The following example form gives a suggested list of questions and notes from observations.

Questions to ask parents about the child's ability to communicate

Questions to ask parents	Parent's response or observations
Name of parent and relationship to child	
Name of child	
Date form is completed	
Preferred language of the child	
View of parent of child's ability in preferred language	
View of parent of child's ability in English	
Stories and rhymes that the child likes in home language	
Other favourite activities, toys or materials	

It is also helpful to have some key words that the child uses and understands. The following table gives some ideas on how to collect key words in order to support communication with the child. The Key Person may need to consider words and phrases that are useful to know in the setting such as 'toilet', 'home time', 'dinner', 'sleep' or 'thirsty'? However. it is also important to ask parents for key words that they think their child may need to use or understand.

Key words with translation into English and pronunciation

Key word	Child (tick as needed)		Pronunciation (write it how it is said)	Translation into English
	Uses this word	Understands this word		

It is also important that that the Key Person shares the nursery's statement, based on the EYFS (see Chapter 3), on supporting children learning EAL. This will help prevent concerns or misunderstandings occurring later. A common misunderstanding can occur when the parent or the setting supports an English-only approach to learning in the setting. It is important to remember that this is detrimental to the child's proficiency in both their home language and English, and can affect the child's self-esteem as well.

Denholm Nursery cont'd from p12

During the home visit, the parent expresses a concern about their child learning English at such a young age. This is because the grandmother lives in the family home and only speaks Polish. The grandmother has already disapproved of the parents sending their child to Denholm Nursery, so they wanted to make sure that the child could continue to communicate in Polish to his/her grandmother.

REFLECTION POINT

What would you do at this point if you were the Key Person on the home visit?

The Key Person reassures the parent that they would be encouraging the child to use Polish within the setting and the setting would wherever possible support the child to improve the way she communicated in Polish too. The Key Person explained further that the learning of English was in addition to Polish and would not replace it – indeed, it would be important for the child's overall development to continue to use Polish at home wherever possible. The Key Person takes the opportunity to talk about how they 'teach' the child in the setting to read and learn about numbers, so that from the outset there was a shared expectation of the best way for the child to learn. The parents appreciated the time the Key Person took to explain this, as it was different to the way that they had been taught.

As with all children, it is important that as much information as possible is shared both ways between parents and the setting to ensure that the child's transition is as smooth as possible. The EYFS states:

'3.72 Providers must make the following information available to parents and/or carers:

- how the EYFS is being delivered in the setting, and how parents and/or carers can access more information (for example, via the DfE website);

- the range and type of activities and experiences provided for children, the daily routines of the setting and how parents and carers can share learning at home;

- how the setting supports children with Special Educational Needs and disabilities;

- food and drinks provided for children;

- details of the provider's policies and procedures (all providers except childminders must make copies available on request) including the procedure to be followed in the event of a parent and/or carer failing to collect a child at the appointed time, or in the event of a child going missing at, or away from, the setting;

- staffing in the setting; the name of their child's key person and their role; and a telephone number for parents and/or carers to contact in an emergency.'

(DfE, 2012, p.27)

Stage 3: The child arrives at the setting

Once the child arrives, it is important to remember all the normal processes for helping a child to settle in. This includes encouraging parents to stay in the room for the first few visits and taking a flexible approach. The Key Person will:

- have prepared some activities and toys that she knows the child likes;

- have found some familiar objects to help the child settle in;

- have a ready smile and some key words to create a sense of comfort and familiarity;

- find a buddy for the child who either shares the same language and/or has strong social skills;

- have a quiet cosy area for the child to chill out – it can be very tiring to be in a new environment;

- endeavour to spend some time outdoors;

- ensure quality time with the Key Person and the back-up (limit the amount of adults the child is having contact with in the early stages of induction);

- allow time for the child to respond and to be silent;

- make a welcome book with the child to take home and share with the family, for example, photos of the child's key people, new room and their buddy and any pictures they may have done.

The support of the rest of the team in the room is important to help the Key Person spend time settling the new child. It is important to remember that the child will need a continued level of support for the next few days and weeks.

Reflecting on supporting children learning EAL so that they feel happy and settled at the setting

In order to help a child to feel comfortable in the setting, do you:

- Collect information relevant to all children, for example, what they like to play with, what their favourite songs and stories are and how they like to be comforted?

- Know how to pronounce and spell the children's and parent's names correctly?

And, have you:

- Given parents an opportunity to share their wishes with regard to use of their home language and shared the policy or statement on supporting children learning EAL?

- Reviewed your environment to include pictures of families from different backgrounds, representation of different scripts and resources relevant to the child, both a favourite toy and resources of cultural significance?

- Discussed how the family would like to be communicated with, for example, email, through a family friend or a daily diary sheet?

- Asked another parent at the setting to befriend the family in order to support transition?

- Shared your parent partnership/Key Person policy to reinforce what the parents can expect from the nursery and the nursery's expectations of the parents as well?

- Let parents know that the child can bring in familiar/comforting resources from home?

- Asked about any cultural differences, for example, use of knives and forks, encouraging independence?

- Considered the option of translation, and how to go about this effectively whilst maintaining the family and child's confidentiality?

Do all the practitioners in the room/setting:

- Have a good understanding of the induction information gathered, for example, have they learnt the key words or how to pronounce the child's name?

- Need any additional training to implement the nursery policies shared with the parents?

- Use non-verbal communication well, for example, do they have a comforting tone of voice? Do they use positive expressions?

CHAPTER 3

EAL and the EYFS

This chapter considers the role of the Statutory Framework for the EYFS (DfE 2012) and the requirements in relation to children learning EAL. This is then considered in relation to other guidance, and practical steps are identified to achieve these requirements. This chapter endS with questions to aid reflection on practice in relation to the Statutory Framework for the EYFS.

The EYFS framework became mandatory for all early years providers from 1 September 2012. This includes maintained schools, non-maintained schools, independent schools and all providers on the Early Years Register. Thus, the scope of the framework includes those who work in the private, voluntary and independent sectors as well as childminders. Learning and development requirements are given legal force by an Order made under Section 39(1)(a) of the Childcare Act 2006. Safeguarding and welfare requirements are given legal force by Regulations made under Section 39(1)(b) of the Childcare Act 2006. The framework contains:

■ an introduction which includes the overarching principles of the EYFS;

■ the learning and development requirements including assessment;

■ safeguarding and welfare requirements.

The aims of the EYFS were discussed briefly in Chapter 2 and are relevant to when considering children learning EAL. The EYFS seeks to provide:

■ quality and consistency in all early years settings, so that every child makes good progress and no child gets left behind;

■ a secure foundation through learning and development opportunities, planned around the needs and interests of each individual child and assessed and reviewed regularly;

■ partnership working between practitioners, and with parents and/or carers;

■ equality of opportunity and anti-discriminatory practice, ensuring that every child is included and supported.

(EYFS, DfE 2012, p.2)

These are important points to consider. In 2009, the EYFSP (Department for Children Schools and Families (DCSF), 2010) results showed that:

'54% of children whose first language was English achieved six or more points in each of the seven scales in Personal, Social, Emotional Development (PSED) and Communication, Language and Literacy development (CLL) compared to 42% of children whose first language is other than English. The percentage of children gaining this score overall was 52%. Primary National Strategy, 2007 reminds practitioners that whilst '…the skills, knowledge and understanding of children learning English as an additional language (EAL) are often underestimated. This makes it more likely that they will be vulnerable to poor Foundation Stage Profile outcomes.'

This data illustrates a need to ensure that there is quality and consistency for all children including those learning EAL, and that all children are included and supported. The EYFS Development Matter Guidance highlights four principles that should guide practice in early years settings:

■ every child is a unique child, who is constantly learning and can be resilient, capable, confident and self-assured;

■ children learn to be strong and independent through positive relationships;

■ children learn and develop well in enabling environments, in which their experiences respond to their individual needs and there is a strong partnership between practitioners and parents and/or carers;

■ children develop and learn in different ways and at different rates. The framework covers the education and care of all children in early years provision, including children with Special Educational Needs and disabilities.

Within the learning and development requirements there is specific guidance for children learning EAL. The EYFS states:

'1.8 For children whose home language is not English, providers must take reasonable steps to provide opportunities for children to develop and use their home language in play and learning, supporting their language development at home. Providers must also ensure that children have sufficient opportunities to learn and reach a good standard in English language during the EYFS, ensuring children are ready to benefit from the opportunities available to them when they begin Year 1. When assessing communication, language and literacy skills, practitioners must assess children's skills in English. If a child does not have a strong grasp of English language, practitioners must explore the child's skills in the home language with parents and/or carers, to establish whether there is cause for concern about language delay.'

This requirement will now to be considered in detail to pick out the following key messages.

> 1 **Providers must take reasonable steps to provide opportunities for children to develop and use their home language in play and learning at the setting.**

This means that providers need to find out about children's home languages when the child starts in a setting (see Chapter 2). Then there is an emphasis on the practitioners to encourage the child to use their home language in the setting. This can be done through:

- buddying-up children who speak the same language to play together;

- practitioners using some key words of the child's home language to encourage its use in the setting;

- practitioners encouraging children to say things in different languages, in order to show an acceptance of different languages;

- providing representations of different languages in the setting, both written and verbal.

> 2 **Providers must support children whose home language is not English in their language development at home.**

This means that providers have to be aware of the languages that children speak or understand at home. They also need to talk to parents about their policy or statement on supporting children who are learning

EAL. The earlier this statement is discussed with parents the less likely there are to be problems or misunderstandings. It is important to be clear in the policy or statement on the use of home languages and English in the setting and in the home, and how both are seen as important.

The following key principles from Supporting Children Learning EAL (Primary National Strategy, 2007), alongside the requirements of the EYFS, may be helpful as a starting point for a policy or statement on supporting children learning EAL. These are:

> - Bilingualism is an asset and the first language has a continuing and significant role in identity, learning and the acquisition of additional languages.
>
> - Supporting continued development of first language and promoting the use of first language for learning enables children to access learning opportunities within the EYFS and beyond through their full language repertoire.
>
> - Cognitive challenge can and should be kept appropriately high through the provision of linguistic and contextual support.
>
> - Language acquisition goes hand in hand with cognitive and academic development, with an inclusive curriculum as the context.

In their guidance on supporting children learning EAL, the Primary National Strategy recognises that the need to talk to parents about how important their home language is:

'Children need to develop strong foundations in the language that is dominant in the home environment, where most children spend most of their time. Home language skills are transferable to new languages and strengthen children's understanding of language use.'

(Primary National Strategy, 2007, p.4)

3 Providers must also ensure that children have sufficient opportunities to learn and reach a good standard in English language during the EYFS, ensuring children are ready to benefit from the opportunities available to them when they begin Year 1.

This requirement ensures that children receive a balanced approach to language development. There may be a temptation to interpret this to mean that the best approach is to only allow English to be spoken, however:

'Developing and maintaining a home language as the foundation for knowledge about language will support the development of English and should be encouraged. Insistence on an English-only approach to language learning in the home is likely to result in a fragmented development where the child is denied the opportunity to develop proficiency in either language. The best outcome is for children and their families to have the opportunity to become truly bilingual with all the advantages this can bring.'

(Primary National Strategy, 2007, page 4)

This demonstrates the need for both the child's home language and English to be used throughout the EYFS, from birth to the end of the year the child is five.

There are a number of things practitioners can do to support children in learning EAL, as suggested by Primary National Strategy, 2007. Practitioners can:

- Encourage children to have time to play and explore together in activities such as role-play where interaction is more likely to take place, or where there are shared resources.

- Observe what the child says and understands in English and in their home language and use the observations to help plan support for language. Observations can include noticing the parts of English the child finds difficult or challenging and setting up opportunities to use this. An example may be the use of 'he' and 'she', and so the practitioner may plan to ensure there are boy and girl dolls to play with and talk about, or family photographs to share.

- Talk and model how to say certain phrases or words that the child is using or is unsure of.

- 'Recast' when a child makes a mistake in English by merely acknowledging what the child said and then saying it in the correct way. So if a child said 'I sawed some sheeps', then the practitioner can say ' That's lovely, you saw some sheep at the farm.'

- Use statements rather than questions where the child can feel under pressure to respond in a certain way. So instead of asking 'What colour is the car?' the practitioner talks about the car in simple terms, 'I like your car, it looks good.'

- Model self-talk in English. This can be a useful way of helping a child hear English used. This is particularly helpful when engaged in a routine activity or experience as it gives an opportunity to build up English vocabulary. However, it should not be unending!

- Use parallel talk. This is where a practitioner narrates what a child is doing. Again this should not be done for too long or all the time but can be useful at times.

- Pair or group a child learning EAL with a child or children who are competent in English. This can be helpful, but remember it will be tiring for the child learning EAL and they may need a brain break!

4 When assessing communication, language and literacy skills, practitioners must assess children's skills in English.

This indicates that practitioners need to observe the child's abilities in English. However, the principle of building parental partnerships is emphasised in the guidance on the EYFS progress-check at age two, NCB, 2012.

CASE STUDY

Abdi is two years and nine months old and has been attending a pre-school setting three mornings a week for a few months. His home language is Somali. The practitioner sensitively organises the feedback session for the parents and explains to them the importance of Abdi continuing to speak Somali at home. She uses this as an opportunity to ask about how well Abdi speaks Somali at home.

The best approach is to collect formative assessment such as observations and samples of the child's talk in the languages the child speaks and understands. It can also be helpful to look at the child's record of learning and development with the child and note what the child says and the language used.

5 If a child does not have a strong grasp of English language, practitioners must explore the child's skills in the home language with parents and/or carers to establish whether there is cause for concern about language delay.

The final part of this learning and development requirement indicates the need to consider the child's strengths and difficulties across all areas of learning and development. It is important when discussing a child's abilities with his/her parents that this is done with sensitivity and care. There are some helpful prompt questions to ask parents, as shown in Chapter 2, when a child first starts at a setting. There is more guidance on working with children learning EAL and Special Educational Needs, in Chapter 10.

Reflecting on supporting children learning EAL in terms of the EYFS framework (DfE, 2012)

Give three examples of practice to demonstrate the following:

- The ways you provide opportunities for children to develop and use their home language through play and learning.

- The methods you are taking to support children in their language development at home.

- The opportunities you are creating to help children learning EAL to learn and achieve a good standard in English language.

- Where your assessments (summative and formative) identify their communication, language and literacy skills in English.

- If a child does not have a strong grasp of English language, how are you exploring the communication, language and literacy skills in the home language?

- How you work to ensure that you are assessing whether there is cause for concern about language delay for children learning EAL.

CHAPTER 4

Supporting children in the prime areas of learning and development

This chapter considers the statements within the prime areas of learning and development in Development Matters non-statutory guidance for the EYFS. The key guidance for supporting children learning EAL is identified and key questions generated to support practitioners in reflecting upon their practice and the environment.

What are the prime areas of learning and development?

The prime areas of learning and development are stated in the EYFS requirements (DfE 2012). The framework identifies seven areas and states that all are important and interconnected. Three areas are identified as prime areas as these are:

'particularly crucial for igniting children's curiosity and enthusiasm for learning, and for building their capacity to learn, form relationships and thrive.'

(EYFS, DfE 2012, p.4)

They are viewed as the 'basis for successful learning in the four specific areas.'

The three prime areas of learning and development are:

- Communication and Language
- Physical Development
- Personal, Social and Emotional Development

The EYFS outlines the educational programmes that must be delivered for these areas of learning and development. This involves the activities and experiences for the children from birth to the year they are five and are as follows:

> Communication and language development involves giving children opportunities to experience a rich language environment; to develop their confidence and skills in expressing themselves; and to speak and listen in a range of situations.

> Physical Development involves providing opportunities for young children to be active and interactive, and to develop their coordination, control and movement. Children must also be helped to understand the importance of physical development.

> Personal, Social and Emotional Development involves helping children to develop a positive sense of themselves, and others; to form positive relationships and develop respect for others; to develop social skills and learn how to manage their feelings; to understand appropriate behaviour in groups; and to have confidence in their own abilities.

Practitioners working with younger children within the EYFS are expected to focus strongly on these three prime areas. As the children grow older the balance is expected to shift to incorporate the four specific areas; Literacy, Mathematics, Understanding the World and Expressive Arts and Design. Each area has to be implemented through play and a balance of adult-led and child-initiated activity. These requirements are in place for all children, including those learning EAL.

Communication and Language

This area of learning and development is divided into three aspects in the EYFS:

- Listening and attention
- Understanding
- Speaking

It is vital to remember that practitioners supporting children learning EAL will need to develop the language and communication of all the children and what is good practice for all of the children is good practice for children learning EAL! It is important to look beyond the age band of the children you work with and consider practice and developments in the environment that are helpful in other age bands. It can be useful to consider the child's developmental age band in English and consider the guidance for practice (positive relationships) and the environment (enabling environments) to help reflect on practice.

In listening and attention, while all the statements in the age bands birth to 11 months, eight-20 months and 16 to 26 months are relevant to children learning EAL there is no specific reference to children learning EAL until the 22-36 months age band. Indeed, all of the guidance for practitioners in the aspect of listening and attention has high relevance for children learning EAL. Similarly, in both speaking and understanding there are different amounts of specific guidance. This is detailed in the following tables.

Communication and Language: Listening and attention

Age band	Positive Relationships: what adults could do	Enabling Environments: what adults could provide
22 – 36 months	Be aware of the needs of children learning EAL from a variety of cultures and ask parents to share their favourites from their home languages.	Encourage children to learn one another's names and to pronounce them correctly. Ensure all staff can pronounce the names of children, parents and other staff members. Make sure that shortened names and nicknames are not substituted instead.
30 – 50 months	Share rhymes, books and stories from many cultures, sometimes using languages other than English, particularly where children are learning EAL. All children will then hear a range of languages and recognise the skill needed to speak more than one.	
40 – 60 months	Ask parents to record regional variations of songs and rhymes. Give children opportunities both to speak and to listen, ensuring that the needs of children learning English as an additional language are met, so that they can participate fully.	

Source: Early Education, 2012, pp.15-16

Communication and Language: Understanding

Age band	Positive Relationships: what adults could do	Enabling Environments: what adults could provide
Birth – 11 months		Display lists of words from different home languages and invite parents and other adults to contribute.
8 – 20 months		Include languages such as Romany and Creole, since seeing their languages reflected in the setting will encourage all parents to feel involved and valued.
16 – 26 months	Recognise young children's competence and appreciate their efforts when they show their understanding of new words and phrases.	
30 – 50 months	When introducing a new activity, use mime and gesture to support language development. Showing children a photograph of an activity such as hand washing helps to reinforce understanding. Be aware that some children may watch another child in order to know what to do, rather than understanding it themselves.	Help children to predict and order events coherently by providing props and materials that encourage children to re-enact situations using talk and action. Find out from parents how children make themselves understood at home; confirm which their preferred language is.

Source: Early Education, 2012, pp.17-18

Communication and Language: Speaking

Age band	Positive Relationships: what adults could do	Enabling Environments: what adults could provide
Birth – 11 months	Find out from parents how they like to communicate with their baby, noting especially the chosen language. Ensure parents understand the importance of talking with babies in their home language. Communicate with parents to exchange and update information about babies' personal words.	Learn and use key words in the home languages of babies in the setting. Provide tapes and tape recorders so that parents can record familiar, comforting sounds, such as lullabies in home languages. Use these to help babies settle if they are tired or distressed.
8 – 20 months	Try to 'tune in' to the different messages young babies are attempting to convey. Find out from parents greetings used in English and languages other than English and use them in the setting. Recognise and equally value all languages spoken and written by parents, staff and children.	Find out from parents the words that children use for things which are important to them, such as 'bankie' for their comfort blanket, remembering to extend this question to home languages. Explain that strong foundations in a home language support the development of English.
16 – 26 months	Accept and praise words and phrases in home languages, saying English alternatives and encouraging their use. Encourage parents whose children are learning English as an additional language to continue to encourage use of the first language at home. Support children in using a variety of communication strategies, including signing, where appropriate.	Plan to talk through and comment on some activities to highlight specific vocabulary or language structures, e.g. 'You've caught the ball. I've caught the ball. Nasima's caught the ball'. Provide stories with repetitive phrases and structures to read aloud to children to support specific vocabulary or language structures.
22 – 36 months	Follow the child's lead to talk about what they are interested in.	Plan to encourage correct use of language by telling repetitive stories, and playing games which involve repetition of words or phrases.
30 – 50 months	Give children 'thinking time.' Wait for them to think about what they want to say and put their thoughts into words, without jumping in too soon to say something yourself. For children learning English as an additional language, value non-verbal communications and those offered in home languages. Add words to what children say, e.g. child says 'Brush dolly hair', you say 'Yes, Lucy is brushing dolly's hair.'	Provide opportunities for children whose home language is other than English, to use that language. Help children to build their vocabulary by extending the range of their experiences.

Source: Early Education, 2012, pp.19-21

It is noticeable in these tables that other aspects have been selected beyond those that specifically mention supporting children with EAL or use of home languages. This is because it is important to recognise ways of supporting children's language development are universal.

Reflecting on Practice in supporting children learning EAL in Communication and Language:

In supporting children's listening and attention do you:

- Ask parents to share their favourite stories, rhymes and songs from their home languages?
- Share rhymes, books and stories from many cultures?
- Share rhymes, books and stories in languages other than English?
- Ask parents to record songs and rhymes in different languages and dialects?
- Give children learning EAL opportunities both to speak and to listen as much as their peers?
- Encourage children to learn one another's names and to pronounce them correctly?
- Ensure all staff can pronounce the names of children, parents and other staff members?

In supporting children's understanding do you?

- Recognise young children's competence when they show an understanding of new words?
- Appreciate children's efforts in trying to understand new words and phrases?
- Use mime and gesture when introducing a new activity to support language development?
- Have photographs of activities, such as tidying up toys, to reinforce understanding?
- Give instructions to children in small groups or pairs so they can watch each other to know what to do?

In supporting children's speaking do you:

- Find out from parents how they, and other members of the family, communicate with their child, noting the chosen language?
- Talk to parents about the importance of continuing to use home language with children learning EAL?
- Communicate with parents to exchange and update information about children's personal words including those in home language?
- Try to 'tune in' to the communication intended by each child even when it is in home language?
- Find out from parents greetings used in languages other than English?
- Use the greetings that families and children use in home languages in the setting?
- Accept and praise words and phrases children say and use in home languages?
- Model the English alternatives to home language words and sensitively encourage their use?
- Support children in using a variety of communication strategies?
- Follow the child's lead and talk about what they are interested in?
- Give children 'thinking time' rather than giving the words and ideas too quickly?
- Value children's communication in all it's possible forms including non-verbal communications and home languages?
- Develop children's language further by add one or two words to what children say, for example, the child says 'my car', you say 'Yes, the big car'?

In terms of the environment supporting children learning EAL do you have?

- Displays of words from different home languages that parents and other key adults have contributed to?
- The languages spoken by all the staff, families and children who attend the setting in speaking and in writing?
- Props and materials that encourage children to re-enact familiar events or experiences?
- Photographs that support children in anticipating the routine and order of the day?
- A record of the language(s) the children's prefer to use at home?
- Staff using key words in home language that children are likely to understand?
- Recording and play-back devices containing parents' sounds, rhymes, stories or lullabies?
- Have a setting policy or statement that explains that strong foundations in a home language support the development of English?
- Stories and songs with repetitive phrases and structures to read aloud to children to support specific vocabulary or language structures?
- A range of opportunities for children learning EAL to use their home language in the setting?
- Plan and offer a wide range of experiences for children to build their vocabulary?

Physical Development

This area of Learning and Development is divided into two aspects in Development Matters in the EYFS:

- Moving and handling
- Health and self-care

It is vital to remember that practitioners supporting children learning EAL will need to develop the physical skills of all the children and what is good practice for all of the children is good practice for children learning EAL.

The Development Matters statements that are particularly relevant to children learning EAL are within Health and Self-care rather than Moving and Handling. This does not mean children learning EAL do not have specific needs but these are likely to be linked to how practitioners communicate with children about the expectations, experiences and activities offered within Physical Development. Therefore many of the points about effective communication have been covered within Communication and Language and relate to supporting children's understanding.

There are some specific Development Matters statements that are highly relevant for children learning EAL and these have been selected to help practitioners consider how best to support these children.

Physical Development: Health and self-care

Age band	Positive Relationships: what adults could do	Enabling Environments: what adults could provide
Birth – 11 months	Talk to parents about the feeding patterns of young babies. Discuss the cultural needs and expectations for skin and hair care with parents prior to entry to the setting, ensuring that the needs of all children are met appropriately and that parents' wishes are respected.	Plan to take account of the individual cultural and feeding needs of young babies in your group. There may be considerable variation in the way parents feed their children at home. Remember that some parents may need interpreter support..
8 – 20 months	Talk to parents about how their baby communicates needs. Ensure that parents and carers who speak languages other than English are able to share their views. Help children to enjoy their food and appreciate healthier choices by combining favourites with new tastes and textures.	
16 – 26 months	Be aware of and learn about differences in cultural attitudes to children's developing independence. Discuss cultural expectations for toileting, since in some cultures young boys may be used to sitting rather than standing at the toilet.	
22 – 36 months	Support parents' routines with young children's toileting by having flexible routines and by encouraging children's efforts at independence. Support children's growing independence as they do things for themselves, such as pulling up their pants after toileting, recognising differing parental expectations.	Display a colourful daily menu showing healthy meals and snacks and discuss choices with the children, reminding them, e.g. that they tried something previously and might like to try it again or encouraging them to try something new. Be aware of eating habits at home and of the different ways people eat their food, e.g. that eating with clean fingers is as skilled and equally valued as using cutlery.
30 – 50 months		Provide a cosy place with a cushion and a soft light where a child can rest quietly if they need to.
40 – 60 months	Be sensitive to varying family expectations and life patterns when encouraging thinking about health.	

Source: Early Education, 2012, pp.25-27

It is noticeable in these tables that Development Matters statements have been selected for cultural reasons. This is because it is important as it is vital to understand a child's cultural background in order to best support their development in the setting.

In supporting children's health and self-care, do you:

- Talk to parents about their child's cultural needs for skin and hair care to ensure these needs are met? (See Chapter 2 for an example of a child and family record.)

- Talk to parents about their child's feeding and preferences so you know the food and drink their child is familiar with?

- Talk to parents about how their child communicates?

- Talk to parents about their expectations of their child in terms of independence in relation to eating, drinking, dressing and toileting?

- Find out how children eat at home so that there is an understanding of how the child may eat best at the setting?

- Maintain sensitivity to different family patterns in relation to health, independence and self-care?

In terms of the environment supporting children learning EAL do you have:

- Records such as child biographies showing the type of food each child is familiar with and how they eat at home?

- Communicate about the daily menus and snacks in a way that children learning EAL can understand? For example, do you have pictures and photographs of food and drink?

- Have places where children can relax and rest away from the heavy language demands of the setting?

- A record of the cultural needs of each of the children in terms of diet, self-care and independence?

Personal, Social and Emotional Development (PSED)

This area of Learning and Development is divided into three aspects in Development Matters in the EYFS:

- Making Relationships

- Self-confidence and self-awareness

- Managing feelings and behaviour

It is vital to remember that practitioners supporting children learning EAL will need to develop the personal, social and emotional skills of all the children, and what is good practice for all of the children is good practice for children learning EAL.

There are some specific Development Matters statements for supporting children learning EAL in PSED, but many of the statements that apply to all children are relevant. The ones that have been selected in the tables that follow are particularly useful to consider when supporting children learning EAL.

Some of the statements selected here relate to children with Special Educational Needs (SEN). It is important to be clear that children learning EAL are not children with SEN, but that while some children learning EAL may have SEN, these are different needs. However, some of the approaches that are supportive of children with SEN are also useful for children learning EAL, and indeed for all children. This is largely because some strategies for children with SEN enhance ways of communicating beyond spoken English, such as using visual communication, for example, photographs, and these approaches are particularly helpful for children learning EAL.

Personal, Social, Emotional Development – Making Relationships

Age band	Positive Relationships: what adults could do	Enabling Environments: what adults could provide
Birth – 11 months	Ensure the Key Person or buddy is available to greet a young baby at the beginning of the session, and to hand them over to parents at the end of a session, so the young baby is supported and communication with parents is maintained..	Ensure the Key Person is paired with a 'buddy' who knows the baby and family and can step in when necessary.
8 – 20 months	Follow the baby's lead by repeating vocalisations, mirroring movements and showing the baby that you are 'listening' fully..	Share knowledge about languages with staff and parents and make a poster or book of greetings in all languages use within the setting and the community.
16 – 26 months	Give your full attention when young children look to you for a response.	Play name games to welcome children to the setting and help them get to know each other and the staff.
22 – 36 months	Ensure that children have opportunities to join in.	Create areas in which children can sit and chat with friends, such as a snug den and cosy spaces.
30 – 50 months	Support children in developing positive relationships by challenging negative comments and actions towards either peers or adults. Encourage children to play with a variety of friends from all backgrounds, so that everybody in the group experiences being included.	Provide a role-play area with materials reflecting children's family lives and communities. Consider including resources reflecting lives that are unfamiliar to broaden children's knowledge and reflect an inclusive ethos.
40 – 60 months	Model being a considerate and responsive partner in interactions. Be aware of and respond to particular needs of children who are learning English as an additional language.	Ensure that children have opportunities over time to get to know everyone in their group, not just their special friends.

Source: Early Education, 2012, pp.8-9

Personal, Social, Emotional Development – Self-confidence and self-awareness

Age band	Positive Relationships: what adults could do	Enabling Environments: what adults could provide
Birth – 11 months	Respond to and build on babies' expressions, actions and gestures. Babies will repeat actions that get a positive response from you. Find out what babies like and dislike through talking to parents.	Plan to have times when babies and older siblings or friends can be together. Plan time to share and reflect with parents on babies' progress and development, ensuring appropriate support is available where parents do not speak or understand English..
16 – 26 months		Making choices is important for all children. Consider ways in which you provide for children with disabilities to make choices, and express preferences about their carers and activities.

22 – 36 months	Be aware of cultural differences in attitudes and expectations. Continue to share and explain practice with parents, ensuring a two-way communication using interpreter support where necessary.	Consult with parents about children's varying levels of confidence in different situations.
30 – 50 months	Encourage children to see adults as a resource and as partners in learning.	Record individual achievements that reflect significant progress for every child.
40 – 60 months	Encourage children to explore and talk about what they are learning, valuing their ideas and ways of doing things.	Provide regular opportunities to reflect on successes, achievements and their own gifts and talents.

Source: Early Education, 2012, pp.10-11

Personal, Social, Emotional Development – Managing feelings and behaviour

Age band	Positive Relationships: what adults could do	Enabling Environments: what adults could provide
Birth – 11 months	Find as much as you can from parents about young babies before they join the setting, so that the routines you follow are familiar and comforting.	Learn lullabies that children know from home and share them with others in the setting. Suggest to parents that they bring something from home as a transitional (comfort) object.
8 – 20 months	Establish shared understandings between home and setting about ways of responding to babies' emotions.	Ensure that children can use their comfort objects from home when in the setting. Share information with parents to create consistency between home and setting so that babies learn about boundaries.
22 – 36 months	Support children's symbolic play, recognising that pretending to do something can help children to express their feelings.	Share policies and practice with parents, ensuring an accurate two-way exchange of information through an interpreter or through translated materials, where necessary.
30 – 50 months	Establish routines with predictable sequences and events. Prepare children for changes in the routine. Share with parents the rationale of boundaries and expectations to maintain a joint approach.	To support children with SEN, use a sequence of photographs to show the routine in the setting. Use pictures or consistent gestures to show children with SEN the expected behaviours. Provide a safe space for children to calm down or when they need to be quiet.
40 – 60 months	Affirm and praise positive behaviour, explaining it makes children and adults feel happier.	Involve children in agreeing codes of behaviour and taking responsibility for implementing them.

Source: Early Education, 2012, pp.12-14

It is noticeable in these tables that other aspects have been selected beyond those that specifically mention supporting children with EAL or use of home languages. This is because it is important to recognise that the ways of supporting children's Personal, Social and Emotional Development are universal.

Reflecting on Practice in supporting children learning EAL in Personal, Social, Emotional Development (PSED)

In supporting children's skills in making relationships, do you:

- As a Key Person, spend time with each Key Child and his/her parents?
- Show the children, including those who are learning EAL that you are listening fully to them?
- Support all the children, including those with EAL, to join in their own way?
- Challenge negative comments and actions to both children and adults?
- Help the children know the names of all the other children and adults in the group?
- Encourage and praise children for playing with a range of different children?
- Respond to the particular needs of children learning EAL in making relationships with others?

In supporting children's self-confidence and self-awareness, do you:

- Respond to children's actions and gestures?
- Talk to parents about what their child likes or dislikes?
- Have an awareness and understanding of different cultural expectations and attitudes?
- Help the children learning EAL to see adults as partners in learning?
- Encourage all the children to share their thoughts and learning with others?

In supporting children to manage their behaviour and feelings, do you:

- Find out from parents about their children's routines so these can be followed in the setting?

- Talk to parents about responding to children's feelings to develop a consistent response?
- Give children opportunities for role-play where the children can act out or try out emotions they may be feeling?
- Routines with predictable events and sequences?
- Warn the children and parents of changes in the routine?
- Share with parents the behaviour expected at the setting to help develop a joint approach?
- Praise and affirm positive behaviour that children display, explaining how it helps make everyone happy?

In terms of the environment supporting children learning EAL do you have:

- A Key Person system where there is a 'buddy' in place who knows the child and family well and can step in when needed?
- Spaces where children can sit and chat with each other, where they can calm down or go to be quiet?
- Have displays of different languages that are used within the setting and community?
- A role-play area that reflects children's families' lives and also includes items that broaden children's knowledge of lives that are unfamiliar to them?
- Times for different aged children and siblings to be together?
- The time and the ability to communicate with parents about their child's development i.e. through use of photographs or a translator?
- Ways children with EAL can express their choices about activities and carers?
- Positive records of achievement for children learning EAL?
- Songs and lullabies that EAL learners may sing at home?
- Transitional objects or comfort items for the children, which serve as a reminder of their home?
- Photographs of the routine to support children learning EAL so that they know what is happening next and with whom?
- Have agreed codes of behaviour that are illustrated with photographs to help all children understand them?

Supporting children in the specific areas of learning and development

CHAPTER 5

This chapter considers the statements within the specific areas of learning and development in Development Matters non-statutory guidance for the EYFS. The key guidance for supporting children learning EAL is identified and key questions generated to support practitioners in reflecting upon their practice and the environment.

What are the specific areas of learning and development?

The specific areas of learning and development are stated in the Learning and Development requirements of the Statutory Framework for the EYFS (DfE 2012). The Statutory Framework for the EYFS identifies seven areas of learning and development, and states that all are important and interconnected. Four areas of learning and development are identified as specific areas as these: 'four specific areas, through which the prime areas are strengthened and applied.' (p.5)

The four specific areas of learning and development are:

- Literacy
- Mathematics
- Understanding the World
- Expressive Arts and Design

The Statutory Framework for the EYFS outlines the educational programmes that must be delivered for these areas of learning and development. This involves the activities and experiences for the children aged birth to the year they are five and are as follows:

Literacy development involves encouraging children to link sounds and letters and to begin to read and write. Children must be given access to a wide range of reading materials (books, poems and other written materials) to ignite their interest.

Mathematics involves providing children with opportunities to develop and improve their skills in counting, understanding and using numbers, calculating simple addition and subtraction problems; and to describe shapes, spaces and measures.

Understanding the World involves guiding children to make sense of their physical world and their community through opportunities to explore, observe and find out about people, places, technology and the environment.

Expressive Arts and Design involves enabling children to explore and play with a wide range of media and materials, as well as providing opportunities and encouragement for sharing their thoughts, ideas and feelings through a variety of activities in art, music, movement, dance, role-play and design and technology.

Source: DfE, 2012, p.5

Practitioners working with the younger children within the EYFS, are expected to focus strongly on the three prime areas of learning and development. As the children grow older the balance is expected to shift to incorporate the four specific areas of learning and development. These requirements are in place for all children including those learning English as an Additional Language (EAL).

There are non-statutory guidance materials for practitioners in the form of Development Matters in the EYFS (Early Education, 2012). This guidance reminds practitioners that:

> 'Children have the right, spelled out in the United Nations Convention on the Rights of the Child, to provision which enables them to develop their personalities, talents and abilities irrespective of ethnicity, culture or religion, home language, family background, learning difficulties, disabilities or gender.'

(Early Education, 2012, p.1)

This strong statement shows the clear intention for all children to be supported and included and explicitly incorporates children learning EAL. In Development Matters in the EYFS, there are three columns:

- A Unique Child: observing what a child is learning
- Positive Relationships: what adults could do
- Enabling Environments: what adults could provide

Each specific area of learning and development will be examined in turn, to review statements and guidance relating to supporting children learning EAL.

Literacy

This area of learning and development is divided into two aspects in Development Matters in the EYFS:

- Reading
- Writing

Reading

It is vital to remember that practitioners supporting children learning EAL will need to develop the literacy skills of all the children, and what is good practice for all of the children is good practice for children learning EAL. Children learning English as an Additional Language may have experience of the way their home language is written, although this will vary. It is vital that the setting values children's attempts to make sense of the written form of their home language due to the longer-term benefits of being bilingual and biliterate, being able to read and write in two languages.

A child's who acquires two or more language systems from birth can also progress to reading those languages simultaneously. As the child's understands that print carries meaning, s/he is able to differentiate between the way symbols sounds and looks and may have the confidence to try early reading. Then the unique look and organisation of the different language scripts can be easily be explored with the support of a knowledgeable adult. Through discussions with parents the practitioner should ask for information about the differences in scripts, if the parents have an understanding themselves and discuss how the child can be supported to read in the home language, if the parent wishes. There may be community groups, other settings or schools that support the child to read their home language alongside the early years setting. As long as the child is taught to understand the similarities and differences then they are often able to learn to read two languages simultaneously.

For a child who develops a second language sequentially, it is more likely that this confidence and understanding in reading comes at a much later stage. Supporting the child to develop the early reading skills such as a 'love' of books while also supporting and developing their home language is vital. This will then later enable the child to read in home language or English.

The Primary National Strategies (2007) guidance on supporting children with EAL identifies the following as key ideas:

- Story sessions bring pleasure and enjoyment, develop the imagination and help children to explore a range of ideas and feelings; they help organise their thoughts and link ideas to knowledge.

- Illustrated sequences, photographs, puppetry and wordless picture sequences give children the opportunity to formulate ideas in their home language which can then be translated into English with appropriate support.

- Opportunities to experience story telling in home languages greatly advantage children learning EAL.

- Stories are helpful for language learning, particularly those with a clear story line, written or told in simple direct language. Repetitive books are particularly useful as they give children the opportunity to hear language sequences they can tune into and rehearse.

- Clear illustrations and other visual support, artefacts, story sacks and props should be used with children learning EAL.

- Homemade books, particularly about familiar settings or objects are popular with children learning EAL as the content is recognisable and both stimulating and supportive of communication.

In Reading, whilst the statements in the age bands Birth to 11 months, 8 – 20 months, 16 – 26 months and 22 – 36 months are relevant to children learning EAL, there is no explicit mention until 30 – 50 months age band. However, there are some specific Development Matters statements that are highly relevant for children learning EAL and these have been selected to help practitioners consider how best to support the needs of these children.

Literacy: Reading

Age band	Positive Relationships: what adults could do	Enabling Environments: what adults could provide
8 – 20 months		Make family books using small photo albums with photos of family members, significant people in the child's life, familiar every day objects.
16 – 26 months		Provide CDs of rhymes, stories, sounds and spoken words. Provide story sacks for parents to take home to encourage use of books and talk about stories.
30 – 50 months	Provide dual language books and read them with all children, to raise awareness of different scripts. Try to match dual language books to languages spoken by families in the setting. Remember not all languages have written forms and not all families are literate either in English or in a different home language. Plan to include home language and bilingual story sessions by involving qualified bilingual adults, as well as enlisting the help of parents.	Provide books containing photographs of the children that can be read by adults and that children can begin to 'read' by themselves. Create an environment rich in print where children can learn about words, e.g. using names, signs, posters. Ensure access to stories for all children by using a range of visual cues and story props.
40 – 60 months	Provide story sacks and boxes and make them with the children for use in the setting and at home. Encourage children to recall words they see frequently, such as their own and friends' names.	Encourage children to add to their first-hand experience of the world through the use of books, other texts and information, and information and communication technology (ICT). Provide story boards and props which support children to talk about a story's characters and sequence of events.

Source: Early Education, 2012, pp.28-29

Writing

As with all children, children learning EAL draw on their own experience of writing around them and what writing is used for in their early mark-making and attempts to write, for example, writing names and logos or letters as well as using the different shapes and sizes of the letters they have seen: 'Bengali children sometimes have horizontal lines in their early writing and Urdu early writers use many curls and dots' (Baker, 2007). Therefore early years practitioners need to understand the writing systems the children they work with have experienced and been exposed to. This will then help the practitioners understand these early attempts to write and to value different forms of emergent writing. At this experimental stage, children learning EAL may mix up the different scripts they are learning about. It is recommended that any marks that are unfamiliar are discussed with parents or someone who knows more about the script they may be using.

Different scripts need to be represented in meaningful contexts within the learning environment, for example, resources labelled in different languages, names of the children translated, food packaging in the role-play area. This allows children learning EAL to see real representations of their home languages in the setting and will enhance the experience of monolingual children by giving them a heightened awareness of language and the similarities and differences between different languages and scripts.

In Writing, there are no Development Matters statements prior to 22 – 36 months and practitioners are re-directed to Communication and Language for further guidance. All the statements within Writing are relevant, but some specific Development Matters statements that are highly relevant for children learning EAL have been selected here to help you consider how best to support the needs of these children.

The statements in the tables below apply to reading and writing within both home language and English, as it is important to support the development of both.

Literacy: Writing

Age band	Positive Relationships: what adults could do	Enabling Environments: what adults could provide
22 – 36 months	Listen and support what children tell you about the marks they make.	Draw attention to marks, signs and symbols in the environment and talk about what they represent. Ensure this involves recognition of English and other relevant scripts. Provide materials which reflect a cultural spread, so that children see symbols and marks with which they are familiar, e.g. Chinese script on a shopping bag.
30 – 50 months	Support children in recognising and writing their own names. Make books with children of activities they have been doing, using photographs of them as illustrations.	Write down things children say to support their developing understanding that what they say can be written down and then read and understood by someone else. Encourage parents to do this as well. Model writing for a purpose, e.g. a shopping list, message for parents, or reminder for ourselves. Provide activities during which children will experiment with writing, for example, leaving a message. Include opportunities for writing during role-play and other activities.
40 – 60 months	Talk to children about the letters that represent the sounds they hear at the beginning of their own names and other familiar words. Support and scaffold individual children's writing as opportunities arise.	Provide word banks and writing resources for both indoor and outdoor play. Provide a range of opportunities to write for different purposes about things that interest children. Resource role-play areas with listening and writing equipment. Ensure that role-play areas encourage writing of signs with a real purpose, e.g. a pet shop.

Source: Early Education, 2012, pp.30-31

In supporting children's reading do you:

- Find out which language scripts are used in the homes of the children who attend the setting and how these scripts work?

- Make family books using small photo albums that include photos of family members and significant people in the child's life that are labelled in relevant home languages and English?

- Make photo books showing familiar every day objects labelled in relevant home language and in English?

- Provide CDs of rhymes, stories, sounds and spoken words in English and home languages?

- Provide story sacks/boxes for parents to take home explaining they can be used in home language and English?

- Read dual language books matched to languages spoken by families in the setting?

- Plan home language and bilingual story sessions involving qualified bilingual adults, and parents?

- Provide a print-rich environment?

- Provide a range of visual cues, story boards and story props to help children understand the stories read or told?

In supporting children's writing do you:

- Talk about marks, signs and symbols in English and other relevant scripts in the environment and what they represent?

- Provide materials that reflect the written language families use at home, so that children see symbols and marks with which they are familiar, for example, newspapers, calendars, numbers?

- Model writing in different scripts?

- Provide material available for children to play and write with that includes different scripts, for example, food packaging in the role-play area?

- Provide activities during which children will experiment with writing?

Mathematics

This area of learning and development is divided into two aspects in Development Matters in the EYFS:

- Numbers

- Shape, space and measure

It is important to know the key words for Mathematics in the children's home languages to help support them in their play and development of understanding mathematical concepts. As with the other areas of learning and development, what is helpful for all children is helpful for those learning English as an Additional language. However, there are some specific Development Matters statements that are helpful to reflect on when supporting children learning EAL with Mathematics. These are shown in the tables below:

Mathematics: Numbers

Age band	Positive Relationships: what adults could do	Enabling Environments: what adults could provide
Birth – 11 months 8 – 20 months	Listen and support what children tell you about the marks they make.	Collect number and counting rhymes from a range of cultures and in other languages. This will benefit all children and will give additional support for children learning English as an additional language.
16 – 26 months	Talk to young children about 'lots' and 'few' as they play. Tell parents about all the ways children learn about numbers in your setting. Have interpreter support or translated materials to support children and families learning English as an additional language.	

22 – 36 months	Encourage parents of children learning English as an additional language to talk in their home language about quantities and numbers.	Provide props for children to act out counting songs and rhymes.
30 – 50 months	Use pictures and objects to illustrate counting songs, rhymes and number stories. Encourage children to use mark-making to support their thinking about numbers and simple problems.	
40 – 60 months+	Give children learning English as additional language opportunities to work in their home language to ensure accurate understanding of concepts.	

Source: Early Education, 2012, pp.32-34

Mathematics: Shape, space and measure

Age band	Positive Relationships: what adults could do	Enabling Environments: what adults could provide
Birth – 20 months		Use story props to support all children and particularly those learning English as an additional language.
16 – 26 months	Talk to children as they play with water or sand to encourage them to think about when something is full, empty or holds more.	Use pictures or shapes of objects to indicate where things are kept and encourage children to work out where things belong.
22 – 36 months	Use descriptive words like 'big' and 'little' in everyday play situations and through books and stories. Be consistent in your use of vocabulary for weight and mass.	Collect pictures that illustrate the use of shapes and patterns from a variety of cultures, e.g. Arabic designs.
30 – 50 months	Demonstrate the language for shape, position and measures in discussions, e.g. 'sphere', 'shape', 'box', 'in', 'on', 'inside', 'under', long, longer', 'longest', 'short', 'shorter', 'shortest', 'heavy', 'light', 'full' and 'empty.' Find out and use equivalent terms for these in home languages.	

Source: Early Education, 2012, pp.35-36

In supporting children learning EAL, there are two important aspects to consider: the language/key vocabulary used in English for Mathematics should be made available in the relevant home languages, and visual supports should be used to support the children's understanding at all times.

Reflecting on Practice in supporting children learning EAL in Mathematics

In supporting children in numbers, do you:

- Collect counting and number rhymes from a range of cultures?

- Find out and use key words for Mathematics in relevant home languages such as number names from 0 – 20 and above as needed and words for 'lots', 'many', 'less', 'more' and other quantity words?

- Involve parents in understanding how numbers are taught in your setting, using translators as needed?

- Have representations of different number scripts related to the children's experience of number in the home, for example, calendars?

- Use visual prompts to help children learning EAL understand what is asked of them, for example, instructions, number songs?

In supporting children in shape, space and measure, do you:

- Find out and use home language words for different shapes (such as 'circle', 'square', 'shape' etc.), position (such as 'in', 'on', 'in front of', 'behind', 'next to' etc.) and measure (such as 'full', 'empty', 'heavy', 'light' etc.)?

- Encourage staff to use these words consistently to support children's understanding and assess their knowledge?

- Use visual prompts so children know where to put materials when they have finished playing with them?

Understanding the World

This area of learning and development is divided into three aspects in Development Matters in the EYFS:

- People and Communities
- The World
- Technology

There are a wide range of relevant Development Matters statements within the aspect of People and Communities that apply to supporting children learning EAL alongside other children in the setting. Similarly there are some important opportunities to draw on children learning EAL to become the experts and for them to share with other children their knowledge and experiences of the wider world. However, within the aspect of Technology there is less that is specifically relevant to children learning EAL.

It is important to know the key words in the child's home language that relate to the concepts being covered in Understanding the World to help support them in their learning and development. It is also important to create opportunities for first hand, practical experience wherever possible. The Primary National Strategies (2007) guidance on supporting children learning EAL identifies first-hand experiences as a highly-effective context for learning language. A cooking activity, or a trip outside the setting, e.g. to the local shops or further afield, provides valuable opportunities to introduce or develop language which children can utilise in role-play with a supportive adult. First-hand experiences are important for all children, but they have even greater value for children learning EAL. The tables below identify some specific Development Matters statements that are helpful to reflect on when supporting children learning EAL with Understanding the World:

Understanding the World: People and Communities

Age band	Positive Relationships: what adults could do	Enabling Environments: what adults could provide
16 – 26 months	Help children to learn each other's names, e.g. through songs and rhymes. Be positive about differences between people and support children's acceptance of difference. Be aware that negative attitudes towards difference are learned from examples the children witness. Ensure that each child is recognised as a valuable contributor to the group. Celebrate and value cultural, religious and community events and experiences.	Collect stories for and make books about children in the group, showing things they like to do. Provide books and resources which represent children's diverse backgrounds and which avoid negative stereotypes. Make photographic books about the children in the setting and encourage parents to contribute to these. Provide positive images of all children including those with diverse physical characteristics, including disabilities.

22 – 36 months	Talk to children about their friends, their families and why they are important.	Share photographs of children's families, friends, pets or favourite people. Support children's understanding of difference and of empathy by using props such as puppets and dolls to tell stories about diverse experiences, ensuring that negative stereotyping is avoided.
30 – 50 months	Encourage children to talk about their own home and community life and to find out about other children's experiences. Ensure that children learning EAL have opportunities to express themselves in their home language some of the time.	Provide activities and opportunities for children to share experiences and knowledge from different parts of their lives with each other. Invite children and families with experiences of living in other countries to bring in photographs and objects from their home cultures including items from family members living in different areas of the UK and abroad.
40 – 60 months +	Help children and parents to see the ways in which their cultures and beliefs are similar, sharing and discussing practices, resources, celebrations and experiences. Strengthen the positive impressions children have of their own cultures and faiths and those of others in their community by sharing and celebrating a range of practices and special events.	Ensure the use of modern photographs of parts of the world that are commonly stereotyped and misrepresented. Help children to learn positive attitudes and challenge negative attitudes and stereotypes, e.g. using puppets, Persona dolls, stories and books showing different heroes. Visit different parts of the local community, including areas where some children may be very knowledgeable, e.g. Chinese supermarket, local church, elders lunch club, Greek café. Provide role-play areas with a variety of resources reflecting diversity. Share stories that reflect the diversity of children's experiences. Invite people from a range of cultural backgrounds to talk about aspects of their lives or the things they do in their work, such as a volunteer who helps people become familiar with the local area.

Source: Early Education, 2012, pp.35-36

Understanding the World: The World

Age band	Positive Relationships: what adults could do	Enabling Environments: what adults could provide
22 – 36 months	Encourage young children to explore puddles, trees and surfaces such as grass, concrete or pebbles.	Develop the use of the outdoors so that young children can investigate features, e.g. a mound, a path or a wall.
30 – 50 months	Use parents' knowledge to extend children's experiences of the world. Arouse awareness of features of the environment in the setting and immediate local area, e.g. make visits to shops or a park. Introduce vocabulary to enable children to talk about their observations and to ask questions.	Use the local area for exploring both the built and the natural environment. Teach skills and knowledge in the context of practical activities, e.g. learning about the characteristics of liquids and solids by involving children in melting chocolate or cooking eggs.
40 – 60 months +	Use appropriate words, e.g. 'town', 'village', 'road', 'path', 'house', 'flat', 'temple' and 'synagogue', to help children make distinctions in their observations. Encourage the use of words that help children to express opinions, e.g. 'busy', 'quiet' and 'pollution.' Use correct terms so that, e.g. children will enjoy naming a chrysalis if the practitioner uses its correct name.	Give opportunities to record findings in a variety of ways, e.g. drawing, writing, making a model or photographing.

Source: Early Education, 2012 pp.39-40

Understanding the World: Technology

Age band	Positive Relationships: what adults could do	Enabling Environments: what adults could provide
16 – 26 months	Talk about the effect of children's actions, as they investigate what things can do.	Incorporate technology resources that children recognise into their play, such as a camera.
22 – 36 months	Talk about ICT apparatus, what it does, what they can do with it and how to use it safely.	Provide safe equipment to play with, such as torches, transistor radios or karaoke machines.
40 – 60 months +		Provide a range of materials and objects for children to play with that work in different ways for different purposes, e.g. egg whisk, torch, other household implements, pulleys, construction kits and tape recorders.

Source: Early Education, 2012 pp.41 -42

In supporting children in understanding people and communities, do you:

■ Make books about the children's backgrounds and lives using photographs?

■ Provide positive images of all the children?

■ Celebrate and value relevant cultural and community events?

■ Share photographs of children's friends, families, pets and favourite people?

■ Ensure children can talk about their home lives and community in both English and in home language?

■ Invite parents and community members to talk about their home lives in other countries?

■ Visit different parts of the local community that children may be familiar with?

■ Have a wide range of resources in role-play that reflect children's lives?

■ Help parents and children understand different faiths, cultures, communities and practices?

In supporting children in knowledge of the world, do you:

■ Give first-hand experiences of the local environment?

■ Have photographs of the local area to help children talk about what they have seen in English and in home language?

■ Find out and use relevant key words in children's home languages to help them talk about the local community?

In supporting children in technology, do you:

■ Give first-hand experiences of a range of technology?

■ Find out and use relevant key words relating to technology so that children can talk about it in English and in their home languages?

Expressive Arts and Design

This area of learning and development is divided into two aspects in Development Matters in the EYFS:

■ Exploring and Using Media and Materials

■ Being Imaginative

The Primary National Strategies (2007) guidance on supporting children learning EAL identifies that musical activities are particularly valuable for supporting language learning. Simple songs, rhymes and refrains chanted in a rhythmic way are often the vehicle for children's first attempts to articulate an additional language. Sharing songs and rhymes in home languages reinforces similarities in patterns of languages and fosters links between the home and the setting.

As with the specific area of learning and development, Understanding the World, Expressive Arts and Design, it is important to know the relevant key words to support children in discussing their ideas and also to support their understanding. It is also important to give children learning EAL first-hand, practical experience wherever possible, just as it is with all children. The tables on the next page identify some specific Development Matters statements that are helpful to reflect on when supporting children learning EAL with Expressive Arts and Design.

Expressive Arts and Design: Exploring and using media and materials

Age band	Positive Relationships: what adults could do	Enabling Environments: what adults could provide
16 – 26 months	Listen with children to a variety of sounds, talking about favourite sounds, songs and music. Introduce children to language to describe sounds and rhythm, e.g. loud and soft, fast and slow.	Provide a wide range of materials, resources and sensory experiences to enable children to explore colour, texture and space.
22 – 36 months	Help children to listen to music and watch dance when opportunities arise, encouraging them to focus on how sound and movement develop from feelings and ideas.	Invite dancers and musicians from theatre groups, the locality or a nearby school so that children begin to experience live performances. Draw on a wide range of musicians and storytellers from a variety of cultural backgrounds to extend children's experiences and to reflect their cultural Heritages.
30 – 50 months	Introduce vocabulary to enable children to talk about their observations and experiences, e.g. 'smooth', 'shiny', 'rough', 'prickly', 'flat', 'patterned', 'jagged', 'bumpy', 'soft' and 'hard.'	Lead imaginative movement sessions based on children's current interests such as space travel, zoo animals or shadows.

Source: Early Education, 2012 pp.43-44

Expressive Arts and Design: Being Imaginative

Age band	Positive Relationships: what adults could do	Enabling Environments: what adults could provide
16 – 26 months	Show genuine interest and be willing to play along with a young child who is beginning to pretend.	Provide a variety of familiar resources reflecting everyday life, such as magazines, real kitchen items, telephones or washing materials.
22 – 36 months	Observe and encourage children's make-believe play in order to gain an understanding of their interests.	Offer additional resources reflecting interests such as tunics, cloaks and bags.
30 – 50 months	Support children's excursions into imaginary worlds by encouraging inventiveness, offering support and advice on occasions and ensuring that they have experiences that stimulate their interest.	Tell stories based on children's experiences and the people and places they know well.
40 – 60 months+	Introduce descriptive language to support children, e.g. 'rustle' and 'shuffle.'	Extend children's experience and expand their imagination through the provision of pictures, paintings, poems, music, dance and story. Provide opportunities indoors and outdoors and support the different interests of children, e.g. in role-play of a builder's yard, encourage narratives to do with building and mending.

Source: Early Education, 2012 pp.45-46

Reflecting on Practice in supporting children learning EAL in Expressive Arts and Design

In supporting children in exploring and using media and materials, do you:

■ Talk about favourite songs and rhymes including those from languages other than English?

■ Provide a range of materials and media for children to have first-hand practical experiences with?

■ Find out and use key words from the children's home languages that relate to different media and materials exploring sound and music ('loud', 'soft', etc.), colour ('red', 'blue', 'green' etc.), texture ('hard', 'soft', 'bumpy', 'jagged', etc.) and space ('tall', 'flat', 'low', etc.)?

■ Draw on a wide range of musicians and storytellers that use the children's home languages and cultural heritage?

■ Support and develop all children's interests including those learning English as an Additional Language?

In supporting children in being imaginative, do you:

■ Provide a wide range of real life resources for role-play that reflect children's everyday lives?

■ Provide a range of different types of experiences of poems, music, dance and story that reflect children's lives and cultural heritage?

■ Find out about the families and lives of children learning EAL so that these can be used as the basis for role-play and storytelling?

CHAPTER 6

How to observe, assess and plan for children learning EAL

This chapter examines how observation, assessment and planning can be used effectively to support children learning English as an Additional Language. This is discussed through consideration of the purposes of observation, assessment and planning. It gives examples of ways to observe, assess and plan for children learning English as an Additional Language (EAL).

What is observation?

Observation can be a difficult term to define and understand, as it overlaps into the areas of assessment and recording. The Oxford English Dictionary (2012) defines observation as: 'the action or process of closely observing or monitoring something or someone [and] a statement based on something one has seen, heard, or noticed.' This definition connects monitoring and observation, and is a link also made in the EYFS (DCSF, 2008b; DfE, 2012).

Within the current EYFS (DfE, 2012), observation has been highlighted as: 'a key tool for all practitioners who work with babies and young children' (Early Education, 2012). Overall, the EYFS identifies observation as the central way for practitioners formatively to assess young children and babies. Practitioners are encouraged to: 'Observe children as they act and interact in their play, everyday activities and planned activities, and learn from parents about what the child does at home' (Early Education, 2012). This is because within the current EYFS (DfE, 2012), practitioners are encouraged to recognise the importance of observation: 'On going formative assessment is at the heart of effective early years practice' (Early Education, 2012).

Observation is something that practitioners are doing all the time. It results from practitioners and parents looking at and listening to children. It can be confused with assessment, but observation is merely one part of the assessment process; with young children and babies, observation enables assessment to take place. Indeed, not all observations that are recorded need to be part of the assessment process. This is the case with special moments or objects that a child may wish to keep or make note of in their record of learning and development or that a parent wants to add. This can be a photograph of a child in their special dressing-up clothes, a picture the child particularly enjoyed making or simply a leaf the child found outside. These do not need to be assessed formatively using the EYFS to check the child's development and learning, but simply form part of the memories of the journey of learning and development within the child's life.

Similarly, observation needs to be separated from recording. There are many observations that practitioners and parents make that are not written down or recorded. These are moments in time that do not need to be recorded or kept and instead may require an immediate response from the practitioner. An example of this could be when a practitioner sees a child become upset; the practitioner does not record this but immediately responds, drawing on their knowledge of the child and what comforts him/her.

REFLECTION POINT

What are the differences between observation, assessment and recording?

The EYFS (DCSF, 2008b) highlights the following definitions of observation and assessment that include aspects of recording. These definitions may be helpful for this reflection point:

- 'Observation describes the process of watching the children in our care, listening to them and taking note of what we see and hear.'

- 'We assess children's progress by analysing our observations and deciding what they tell us. We also need to find out about children's care and learning needs from their parents and from these we can identify the children's requirements, interests, current development and learning.'

In addition, it can be helpful to reflect on the reasons why observation is used as the main tool for practitioners to assess children's learning and development.

There are other methods that can be used for assessment, and some may be used with older children or adults. These include other methods for assessment such as short tests or exams, or asking children to complete a set sequence of tasks. However, tests and exams are not formative assessment as these are not assessments made over time. Rather, they are assessments that give the child one chance to achieve whatever is being assessed, although they can be used in a formative way as discussed later in this chapter.

There are other problems associated with these forms of assessment. These include a child's attention span or willingness to engage in the assessment process, any feeling of pressure felt by a child, and the fact that a child may perform differently on different days. Alternatively, parents and/or practitioners could be asked to remember what a child can or cannot do. However, without the aid of observations this relies on the parent and/or practitioner having a faultless memory. In comparison, observation is a less stressful approach for both children and practitioners. It allows assessment over time, reduces pressure and reliance on the parent and practitioner's memory and gives opportunities to catch children learning and developing at their best.

It is also worth thinking about other reasons for using observation as a key tool for assessment and planning. There are a number of reasons, including the following that are identified in the Effective Practice article on observation, assessment and planning (DCSF, 2008b):

- Observation identifies the specific care and learning needs of individual children.
- Observation allows practitioners to see a child as an individual.
- Observation enables planning to meet the needs of the children.
- Observation enables practitioners to identify any new skills and abilities children have developed.

- Observation enables practitioners to identify each child's likes and dislikes.
- Observation enables practitioners to recognise how children respond to different situations, care routines or new people.
- Observation illustrates to practitioners those experiences, routines or activities that a child seems to enjoy or to find difficult, and any that seem to make them anxious.
- Observation helps practitioners assess a child's progress.

How can observation be used to support children learning EAL?

When observing any child, it is important to add sufficient detail for the record of the observation to be informative, but not so lengthy that it becomes a burden. Indeed the Statutory Guidance for the EYFS (DfE, 2012) states:

> 'Assessment should not entail prolonged breaks from interaction with children, nor require excessive paperwork. Paperwork should be limited to that which is absolutely necessary to promote children's successful learning and development.'

This is related to assessment and also observations, as they are part of the assessment process. This encourages practitioners to record the information that is relevant. As with all children, this is an important consideration. When observing children learning EAL, it is relevant to note the language used, both by the person speaking to the child and by the child. However, it is important only to add the details needed and not to extend the observation unnecessarily.

The child is likely to respond in different ways depending on the language used with them. For example, if a child has a story read to them in their home language, their response may be different in comparison to hearing a story read in English. Thus, it is important to observe the child's response and note what language the story was read in. Similarly, if a parent shares an observation they have noted at home, it is always worth asking about the language being used. It is also helpful to note the aspects of Communication and Language being used: Listening and Attention, Speaking and Understanding.

An example of a recorded observation is shown below:

> Sabah listened for five minutes to Fatema, her Key Person, reading a photograph book about food in both English and Punjabi. She repeated key words in Punjabi – 'roti', 'daal' and 'doodh.'

This observation notes Sabah's ability to listen and attend to her Key Person, as well as recording the aspects of the reading that took her interest. Although this example relates to aspects of Sabah's communication and language, the same applies for other areas of learning and development. For example, when recording a child's Personal, Social and Emotional Development (PSED), it is helpful to record the three aspects of Making Relationships, Self-confidence and self-awareness, and Managing feelings and behaviour.

A child's PSED will be affected both by the physical indoor/outdoor environment and the emotional environment they are in. The emotional environment is discussed further in Chapter 9. In observations relating to children's PSED it can be helpful to note any influential factors. This may be the presence of objects that the child is familiar with from home, the use of a language one the child is familiar with or if an experience or activity is one the child has done before. An example of this can be seen within the role-play outlined below. Josef may be able to play at a higher level if the objects within the play are familiar to him, from home perhaps, and if he is playing with other children using his home language. This observation could be recorded as:

> Josef often plays in the home corner with his friend Mikey. They are enjoying using the mobile phones to talk to each other in mostly Polish with one or two English words – 'hello', and 'goodbye.'

This observation contains relevant details such as the language the children are choosing to interact in, the words being used in English as well as the items that are supporting and enhancing the children's play. This observation could be placed in both Mikey and Josef's records of learning and development.

REFLECTION POINT

How often does your setting undertake summative assessments for the children? Is it often enough or is it too often? Is it the same for all children?

This will depend on the observation, but you need to include the date of the observation, the languages used and the people who play a role in the learning and development during the observation. There may be other things that you want to include too.

What is assessment?

Assessment plays an important part in:

1   helping parents, carers and practitioners to recognise children's progress;

2   understand the children's needs;

3   planning activities and support for children.

There are different types of assessment; formative assessment, summative assessment and multiagency assessment.

- **Formative assessment**, also known as ongoing assessment, is an integral part of the learning and development process. For formative assessment, practitioners observe children and talk with parents and/or carers to understand each child's achievement, interests and preferences.

- **Multiagency assessments** are used to bring together summative assessments from different agencies to give a holistic view of a child. The most common example is probably through the Common Assessment Framework (CAF), which brings together agencies to identify and support unmet needs of a child.

- **Summative assessment** is: '...a summary of all the formative assessment carried out over a long period and makes statements about the child's progress.'(DCSF, 2008b)

A summative assessment brings together all the formative assessment on a child in a short report and should include information on how the child is developing. Under the EYFS (DfE, 2012), there are two points where it is statutory for a setting review a child's progress and share with parents and/or carers a summative assessment of a child's learning and development:

- the prime areas between the ages of 24 and 36 months for the Progress Check at two years old;

- the prime and specific areas at the end of the EYFS between the ages of 48 to 60 months+ for the EYFS Profile.

The Statutory Framework for the EYFS (DfE, 2012) highlights that parents and/or carers play an active role in assessment in the following ways:

■ contributing observations and other types of formative assessment;

■ being informed about their child's current progress and development through summative assessment;

■ addressing any learning and development needs identified in summative assessments alongside relevant professionals including early years practitioners.

'Effective practitioners pull together the information they gather in their observations to identify aspects of the child's learning and development. This pulling together of information and thinking about what it tells us forms the basis of what is termed "assessment". When we assess we are making a judgement or decision about the child's progress and needs in one or several areas of learning and development.'

(DfES, 2007)

This identifies assessment as the practitioner, ideally the child's Key Person, collating and then analysing the observations of the child completed by a range of practitioners and the parents and/or carers for a summative assessment. This is crucial in allowing practitioners to understand children's progress and making judgements on the child's learning and development. The Statutory Framework for the EYFS (DfE, 2012) states: 'Assessment plays an important part in helping parents, carers and practitioners to recognise children's progress, understand their needs, and to plan activities and support.' However, as noted previously, the Statutory Framework for the EYFS (DfE, 2012) highlights that assessment should be a manageable process where interaction and play with children is prioritised. Assessment is simply a process where observations and any evidence of learning is analysed, rather than conducted as a separate activity.

Summative assessment plays an important role throughout a child's time in an early years setting and should be done on a regular basis (DCSF, 2008b). The idea of assessing regularly is not defined. This means that there is no statutory directive to pull formative assessments together more frequently at the two points that are statutory – namely at age two and at the end of the academic year when the child is five. However, good practice would indicate that this is likely to be needed more frequently, although the

frequency of when summative assessments take place will vary and is best negotiated by the family and the setting. The frequency may vary between children depending on patterns of attendance and level of need.

REFLECTION POINT

How often does your setting undertake summative assessments for the children? Is it often enough or is it too often? Is it the same for all children?

Progress check at age two

Practitioners have to review the progress of a child when s/he is aged between two and three years old and provide parents and/or carers with a short written summary of their child's development in the prime areas (Communication and Language, Physical Development, Personal, Social and Emotional Development) (DfE, 2012) The progress check must:

■ include the child's development in the three prime areas (Communication and Language, Physical Development, Personal, Social and Emotional Development);

■ identify the child's strengths;

■ identify any areas where the child's progress is less than expected;

■ provide a targeted plan to support the child's future learning and development in any areas where there is a concern that a child may have a developmental delay, a special educational need or a disability that may require involving other professionals as needed.

It must describe the activities and strategies the provider intends to adopt, in order to address any issues or concerns and this should include both the home and setting. The progress check at age two is undertaken by the setting where the child spends most time.

Practitioners must discuss with parents and/or carers how the summary of development can be used to support learning at home and when is the most useful time for the progress check to be carried out. Practitioners should encourage parents and/or carers to share information from the progress check with other relevant professionals, including their health visitor or another setting if the child moves.

It is intended that the progress check should inform the Healthy Child Programme health and development review at age two whenever possible (when health visitors gather information on a child's health and development, allowing them to identify any developmental delay and any particular support from which they think the child/family might benefit). Taking account of information from the progress check should help health visitors identify children's needs more accurately and fully at the health review. Providers must have the consent of parents and/or carers to share information directly with other relevant professionals.

The Progress check can include observations of children and assessments in either English or home language. It is important to note the language used in any aspect of the assessment. The following example is given in the *Know How Guide* (NCB, 2012):

Abdi is two years and nine months old and has been attending a pre-school setting for a few months, three mornings a week. His home language is Somali. His mother Hafsa has limited English and seems keen for Abdi to attend the setting. She is not able to speak to the pre-school staff, but sometimes brings a female friend from the Somali community to act as interpreter. His father, Hanand, has good spoken English and brings Abdi to the setting some mornings. He has sometimes asked if Abdi is being taught English at the setting and said that he would like him to speak English as well as possible.

Maria is Abdi's Key Person. She feels that he has settled well and would like to arrange a time to talk about the progress check. She arranges for the family to come in on a morning when Abdi does not normally attend the pre-school, as that is a day when Hanand works a later shift. Maria speaks to Hafsa via her friend and asks her what support she would like at the meeting. Hafsa says that she is happy for Hanand to interpret for her. Maria prepares for the meeting, ensuring that there are plenty of recent photographs of Abdi within his Learning Journey record. When Abdi and his parents arrive, she encourages them to spend a little while looking at the photographs and the ongoing observations in Abdi's Learning Journey. Abdi excitedly points out pictures of him riding a tricycle in the setting's outdoor area, making remarks in Somali to his parents. Maria discusses the comments she has prepared for the progress check, referring regularly to the photographs in Abdi's Learning Journey. Maria explains that she has no concerns about Abdi's development, as it is appropriate for his age, and that she'd like to know more about what Abdi likes to do at home. Hanand asks if they should speak more English to him at home. Maria explains that it is important for Abdi to continue to develop his home language, so they should

continue to speak Somali to him at home. She also asks if they have any concerns about his language when he is speaking in Somali. Maria has borrowed a dual-language copy of Farmer Duck, a book they have been reading at pre-school and asks if they would like to read it to Abdi at home. Abdi seems excited and begins to put the book into his mother's bag. Maria says that she can give them a copy of the progress check in a couple of days.

This example clearly shows that a child with limited English can be developing typically, and that it is important not to assess a child's learning and development in English alone. It also shows the importance of talking with the parents and/or carers of a child learning EAL about the development of their home language at home, and the value of using a child's home language in the setting and at home.

The EYFS Profile

The EYFS Profile (Standards and Testing Agency (STA), 2012) summarises and describes children's attainment at the end of the EYFS. It is based on ongoing observation and assessment in the three prime (Communication and Language, Physical Development, Personal, Social and Emotional Development) and four specific areas of learning (Literacy, Mathematics, Understanding the World, Expressive Arts and Design) and the three learning characteristics (Playing and Exploring, Active Learning, Creating and Thinking Critically).

Assessments should be based primarily on observation of daily activities and events.

Practitioners should focus on the time when a child demonstrates learning spontaneously, independently and consistently in a range of contexts. These assessments should take account of a range of perspectives including those of the child, parents and carers and other adults who have significant interactions with the child.

A completed EYFS Profile consists of 20 items of information: the attainment of each child assessed in relation to the 17 early learning goal (ELG) descriptors, together with a short narrative describing the child's three learning characteristics. For each ELG, practitioners must judge whether a child is meeting the level of development expected at the end of the Reception Year (expected), exceeding this level (exceeding) or not yet reaching this level (emerging).

There are four main uses of EYFS Profile data (STA, 2012):

- To inform parents and/or carers about their child's development against the ELGs and the characteristics of their learning;

- To support a smooth transition to Key Stage 1 by informing the professional dialogue between EYFS and Key Stage 1 teachers;

- To help Year 1 teachers plan an effective, responsive and appropriate curriculum that will meet the needs of all children;

- To provide an accurate national data set relating to levels of child development at the end of the EYFS, which can be used to monitor changes in levels of children's development and their readiness for Key Stage 1 in school at a local and national level.

This illustrates that summative assessments can also be used formatively, as they can inform or guide any future planning. An example of this can be where teachers review the EYFSP to plan for either an individual or a cohort of children in Year 1.

There are three aspects specific to the assessment of children for whom English is not their home language:

- development in their home language;

- development across areas of learning, assessed through their home language and/or English;

- development of English.

So, although within the EYFS Profile the ELGs for Communication and Language and for Literacy must be assessed in relation to the child's competency in English, the remaining ELGs may be assessed in any language – including the child's home language and English. It is helpful to note which language was used and to be able to compare competency in the home language with competency in English, in order to differentiate between a child who needs support in learning English as an Additional Language and a child with Special Educational Needs.

How can assessment be used to support children learning EAL?

The way formative assessment takes place practically is through the Key Person putting together the child's record of learning and development. This includes written observations from a range of practitioners, photographs, audio recording and artefacts from the child's play in the setting such as drawing, paintings or models. Generally, the Key Person will see how

these observation relate to: '... the examples of development in the columns headed "Unique Child: observing what children can do" to help identify where the child may be in their own developmental pathway (assessment)' (Early Education, 2012). This means that

'Development Matters might be used by early years settings throughout the EYFS as a guide to making best-fit judgements about whether a child is showing typical development for their age, may be at risk of delay or is ahead for their age.'

(Early Education, 2012)

This can be related back to the earlier observations on Sabah, Josef and Mikey, which have now been related to the Development Matters in the EYFS as follows:

Observation:

Sabah listened for five minutes to Fatema, her Key Person, reading a photograph book about food in both English and Punjabi. She repeated key words in Punjabi – 'roti', 'daal' and 'doodh.'

Assessment:

Communication and Language: Listening and Attention 22 – 36 months (English and Punjabi)

Speaking 16 – 26 months (Punjabi)

Observation:

Josef often plays in the home corner with his friend Mikey. They are enjoying using the mobile phones to talk to each other in mostly Polish with one or two English words –' hello' and 'goodbye.'

Assessment:

Personal, Social and Emotional Development: Making Relationships 22 – 36 months (Polish)

Understanding the World; People and Communities, 22 – 36 months (English and Polish)

This briefly gives an observation of a child at play, containing all the relevant details. It adds assessment information to show how the child is developing within areas of learning and development, which can then be compared to their age. This then helps identify whether the child is developing as would be anticipated to be typical, is at risk of delay or is ahead for their age. Over time these formative assessments can be used to establish the summative assessment and whether the child is developing as they should. It is important to review assessments of children both in their home language and in English, in order to help identify if the child is simply at the early stages of learning EAL or if the child has Special Educational Needs. This is discussed in greater detail in Chapter 10.

What is planning?

Planning in the EYFS Effective Practice (DCSF, 2008b) is defined as:

'...the next steps in children's development and learning. Much of this needs to be done on the basis of what (has been) found out from our own observations and assessments as well as information from parents.'

This definition highlights the role of planning as part of the cycle of observation, assessment and planning. This means that practitioners have to link their planning to what children are interested in and need to do.

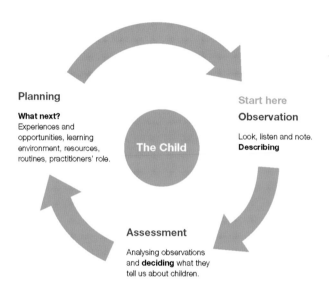

Planning
What next?
Experiences and opportunities, learning environment, resources, routines, practitioners' role.

Start here
Observation
Look, listen and note. **Describing**

The Child

Assessment
Analysing observations and **deciding** what they tell us about children.

DfE (2012) identifies that practitioners must consider the individual needs, interests and stage of development of each child and use this information to plan a challenging and enjoyable experience for each child in all of the areas of learning and development. This should be through the medium of play. Planning should include a mix of adult-led and child-initiated activity to support children's learning and development. Practitioners have to make an ongoing judgement about the balance between activities led by children, and activities led or guided by adults. Over time it is intended that play will become more adult-guided, but remain playful. When observing, assessing and planning for the youngest children, aged birth to three, practitioners are expected to focus strongly on the three prime areas: Communication and Language, Physical Development and Personal, Social and Emotional Development. It is expected that the balance will shift towards a more equal focus on all areas of learning as children grow in confidence and ability within the three prime areas.

The Department for Education states practitioners must reflect on the different ways that children learn when planning and guiding children's activities, and reflect these in their practice (DfE, 2012). The three characteristics of effective teaching and learning are:

■ playing and exploring: children investigate and experience things, and 'have a go';

■ active learning: children concentrate and keep on trying if they encounter difficulties, and enjoy achievements;

■ creating and thinking critically: children have and develop their own ideas, make links between ideas, and develop strategies for doing things.

The Department for Children, Schools and families state there are three possible levels of planning: long-term, medium-term and short-term (DCSF, 2008b).

Long-term planning is intended to provide a structure for covering all the areas of learning and development and the Principles in the EYFS Framework. For example, it can identify how the overall balance of activities is maintained. The balance may relate to:

■ indoor and outdoor play;

■ quiet and lively play;

■ freely-chosen play opportunities through the continuous provision and well-planned, playful, adult-initiated activities.

Medium-term planning gives detail for approximately two to six weeks and tends to focus on groups of children. It may outline:

■ the possible types of experiences and activities appropriate to the age/family group;

■ the outline of daily routines such as feeding times, snack or mealtimes for children, arrival times, provision for outdoor activities as well as indoor, quiet time or times for rest or sleep, time for stories and for group times;

■ the resources needed for room areas such as comfort/ quiet areas, home corners, messy play;

■ access to equipment.

Short-term planning involves daily planning, and is focused more on individual children's needs and how these will be met. It could include the resources needed for the adult-initiated activity of cooking that has arisen from someone's birthday, a festival or another celebration. It can be the removal, adaptation or continuation of an activity included in the continuous provision based on how children have responded in the previous session/s.

How can planning be used to support children learning EAL?

The Department for Education identifies the specific planning needs for children learning English as an Additional Language(DfE, 2012). Practitioners must provide opportunities for children to develop and use their home language in play and learning, and support their language development at home. In addition, children learning EAL need opportunities to learn and use English language during the EYFS.

Examples of how this can be reflected in long-term planning include:

- Developing an induction form that includes a language map showing the different languages used at home (see Chapter 2);

- On a regular basis, reviewing that all children's languages spoken in the setting are represented within the environment in either written form and key words are recorded for staff to use;

- Parent workshops making bilingual story sack that highlight the value of speaking and listening to children at home including the use of home language.

Examples of how this can be reflected within the medium term planning include:

- Planning bilingual story times that reflect the languages spoken and understood by the children in the setting;

- Reviewing the materials in role-play to ensure the resources reflect children's lives and home backgrounds, for example, food packaging in relevant languages;

- Labelling of equipment includes some home language words (written phonetically) to help staff use key words with children;

- Encouraging children who speak the same home language to sit near each other for dinner.

Examples of how this can be reflected within the short-term planning include:

- Adapting the continuous provision to reflect children's interests and enthusiasms, such as having more handbags and keys if these are popular and are creating opportunities for talk;

- Adult-initiated activities that build on observations, such as the discovery that many of the children play alone. This may lead to a small group time using puppets to demonstrate how to children can ask other children to play.

This can be related back to the earlier observations on Sabah, Josef and Mikey, with some suggestions for planning of next steps:

Observation:

Sabah listened for five minutes to Fatema, her Key Person, reading a photograph book about food in both English and Punjabi. She repeated key words in Punjabi – 'roti', 'daal' and 'doodh.'

Assessment:

Communication and Language: Listening and Attention 22 – 36 months (English and Punjabi)

Speaking 16 – 26 months (Punjabi)

Planning:

Medium term: Develop photograph books of the children's families

Short-term: Add relevant cooking items such as milk containers, rice and flour packaging to the role-play area. Encourage staff playing with Sabah to use the key words: 'roti', 'daal' and 'doodh' by putting these on the wall as signs with pictures/photographs.

Observation:

Josef often plays in the home corner with his friend Mikey. They are enjoying using the mobile phones to talk to each other in mostly Polish with one or two English words –' hello' and 'goodbye.'

Assessment:

Personal, Social and Emotional Development: Making Relationships 22 – 36 months (Polish)

Understanding the World; People and communities, 22 – 36 months (English and Polish)

Planning:

Medium term: Increase the space and resources available for role=play so more children can play in the area. Add newspapers and other written materials in Polish to encourage recognition of the language.

Short term: Staff to join play with Mikey and Josef and also speak on the telephone to extend children's spoken language.

Reflecting on observing, assessing and planning for children learning EAL

Do you:

- Observe children speaking, listening or understanding their home language as well as English?

- Assess children in home language where possible?

- Involve parents of children learning English as an Additional Language in the assessment process?

- Plan to develop children's competency in English?

- Plan to develop children's use of home language in the setting?

Have you got:

- Observations in the Learning Journey that reflect the different languages the children listen to, speak and understand?

- Assessments that reflect the child learning English as an Additional language's development in English and in their home language?

Supporting children using the characteristics of effective learning

CHAPTER 7

This chapter examines how the characteristics of effective learning can be identified and used to support practice with children learning English as an Additional Language (EAL). These have been introduced in the revised EYFS (Early Education, 2012, DfE, 2012) and result from the Tickell Review (DfE, 2011).

What are the characteristics of effective learning?

The Statutory Framework for the EYFS (DfE, 2012) identifies that when planning and supporting children's experiences and activities, practitioners must reflect on the different ways that children learn and use this information in their practice. The three characteristics of effective teaching and learning are identified as:

1 playing and exploring – children investigate and experience things, and 'have a go';

2 active learning – children concentrate and keep on trying if they encounter difficulties and enjoy achievements;

3 creating and thinking critically – children have and develop their own ideas, make links between ideas, and develop strategies for doing things.

The characteristics of effective learning were introduced in both the Statutory Framework and Development Matters in the EYFS (Early Education, 2012). The characteristics of effective learning are relevant to all seven areas of learning; the three prime areas (Communication and Language, Physical Development and Personal, Social and Emotional Development) and the four specific areas (Literacy, Mathematics, Understanding the World, Expressive Arts and Design).

The characteristics for effective learning are unique to each child, although there may be some similarities between children. The characteristics for effective learning are not only relevant to early childhood but also for lifelong learning and, within this, Stewart (2011) highlights the importance of how children develop as self-regulated learners.

Self-regulation is most-commonly used in relation to emotions and behaviour. As Stewart identifies, the emotional well-being of children underpins all aspects of learning and development. The three primary strands of self-regulated learning build on the firm foundations of strong relationships and emotional well-being. Stewart identifies these as:

■ Playing and Exploring – children are engaged as agents in their own learning

■ Active Learning – children are motivated to learn

■ Creating and Thinking Critically – children are thinking about their learning

Within Development Matters in the EYFS (Early Education, 2012), the characteristics of effective learning are broken down further, as follows:

Playing and Exploring – engagement is divided into three prompts for observation:

■ Finding out and exploring

■ Playing with what they know

■ Being willing to have a go

Active learning – motivation is divided into three prompts for observation:

■ Being involved and concentrating

■ Keep trying

■ Enjoying achieving what they set out to do

Creating and Thinking Critically – thinking is divided into three prompts for observation:

■ Having their own ideas

■ Making links

■ Choosing ways to do things

It is important to remember that while children may have different characteristics of effective learning, it is the role of the practitioners in the setting to work in ways that promote them and to set an environment that enables effective learning. There is detailed guidance on how adults in early settings can support children in being effective learners in the Positive Relationships column in Development Matters. There are also helpful prompts for adults in setting up the environment to enable children to be effective learners in the Enabling Environment column.

Using the characteristics of effective learning to help plan for children learning EAL

One potential way of using the characteristics of effective learning is through observation of children to develop a profile of what supports children to be effective learners, being engaged, motivated and thinking about what they doing.

Observations of all children can be analysed to show:

- What does the child love to explore?
- What are their favourite activities and experiences?
- What type of play does the child love the most?
- In what type of play will the child try something new?
- What play and activity does the child maintain the most attention in?
- What is the child doing that helps them to keep trying and not give up?
- Who does the child chose to him/her keep on trying?
- When does the child show pride in his/her efforts and achievements?
- When does the child make links between the setting and experiences at home?
- What activities does the child like to do in his/her own way?

These observations indicate the child's preferred activities, experiences, surrounding and people. This can be used as the basis for planning experiences that allow the child time to consolidate and have experiences again, but also indicate where experiences and activities can be adapted slightly to extend children's learning and development.

An example of this is Sanjit, who loves playing with the train set with his friend Raj. He will persist with this activity for long periods of time. He enjoys the building of the track and will spend a longer time on this aspect of the activity than the actual playing with the trains. He and Raj speak in Gujerati to each other as they build. Sanjit likes to build long tracks and will continue even if Raj goes off to play elsewhere, but not for as long as he does with Raj. Sanjit can get upset if other children tread on the track or move it.

This very brief observation indicates what activities engage Sanjit – the train set and the aspect of it he persists with for longer – building the train track. The observation also shows that Raj is a motivating force for Sanjit as he may be playing a role in helping Sanjit to keep trying. Next, practitioners need to consider planning and, at a simple level, this could be to continue to have the train set available for Sanjit as part of the continuous provision. However, to deepen Sanjit's thinking, it may be helpful to partially create a track and then create a problem that Raj and Sanjit could resolve together, such as a block on the line or a need for the track to go from one place to another. This could still be part of the continuous provision or be part of an adult-led activity that a practitioner supports. This could be in a number of ways such as getting alternative resources as needed or giving support for thinking in Gujerati, or a play opportunity where English vocabulary can be supported.

It is important to remember that children learning EAL can be effective learners in the same way as any other child. However, practitioners can't rely on the child telling them in English about what they enjoy or what motivates them or to talk about their thinking. It may relate to taking time to watch, listen and think about what is happening to find patterns in what helps a child learn effectively.

Reflecting upon the characteristics of effective learning for children learning EAL

Stewart utilises self-determination theory to help identify why children learn. She identifies the following psychological needs of children that practitioners need to be mindful of and seek to meet. Children need to:

- be competent
- make sense of what they experience
- have autonomy or control
- be related to others.

She also utilises Bandura's work on self-efficacy, as those with a strong sense of self-efficacy show many of the characteristics of an effective learner. The following demonstrates a motivation to learn:

- to approach challenges as something that can be achieved;
- to become deeply interested and committed to their activities;
- to be resilient and bounce back from difficulties.

This has relevance to all children but it is worth reflecting on practice with those children learning EAL, using the following questions:

- How do I support children learning EAL to feel competent at something at my setting (bearing in mind the child is aware they are less competent than others in communicating in English)?
- How do I support children learning EAL to understand the routines, experiences and activities offered at the setting?
- How do I support children learning EAL to have choice and control?
- How do I support children learning EAL to feel a sense of belonging to their group, their Key Person and the setting?
- How do I support children learning EAL to be willing to have a go at a challenging activity or experience?
- How do I support children learning EAL to become deeply interested and committed to what they are doing?
- How do I support children learning EAL to bounce back and have another go?
- How often do I respond to the interests of children learning EAL in my planning?

It is also helpful to think about how the environment promotes effective learning for children learning EAL:

- Where are open-ended stimulated resources provided in the setting?
- Where are quiet spaces in the setting for the children?
- Which resources are particularly relevant to the children learning EAL?
- Do we find enough time for children to become absorbed and interested in their play?
- How do we record children's efforts as well as their achievements?
- When do we praise children's efforts?
- Are there opportunities for children to find their own ways to represent and develop ideas?
- When is there a 'good choice' for children in terms of play or resources?
- How do we show the children learning EAL the routine of our day?

CHAPTER 8

How can the Key Person approach be used?

This chapter seeks to explore the Key Person approach and how it can be used to support children learning English as an Additional language. It explains how attachment theory underpins the Key Person approach and then examines the Key Person approach in the Early Years Foundation Stage (DfE, 2012). The chapter concludes by considering how the Key Person can develop effective working practices in order to support children learning English as an Additional Language, and their parents.

What is the Key Person approach?

Both the Early Years Learning and Development Review (Evangelou et al., 2009) and literature review for Birth to Three Matters (David et al., 2003) highlight that one of the most important theories of early childhood development for early years practitioners is Bowlby's theory of attachment (1953, 1969, 1973, & 1980). Within Bowlby's theory, attachment is the development of a strong nurturing bond between mother and child during the first few months of life. Ainsworth et al. (1978) argue that this first important attachment relationship or close bond serves to provide the child with a secure emotional base that can have a significant bearing on their future emotional and social development.

Trevarthen (1988) extends the idea of attachment by stating that mothers go beyond being a secure base for their babies and play the role of friend and playmate. Trevarthen developed the concept of 'intersubjectivity', where the shared understanding between mother and child is achieved through recognition and coordination of the communication between them. This is achieved by mother and child having a shared focus of attention and agreement on the nature of how they are going to communicate. In young babies this is likely to be through smiles, gurgles and eye gaze. As the child grows older, language increasingly is used. These key theories of attachment and intersubjectivity have application for practitioners working with young children in early years settings.

The PSED training materials (Sure Start, 2006) explains attachment in terms of forming relationships both within and beyond the family:

'All humans have an inbuilt desire to form an intense emotional tie with a close caregiver. This helps to ensure survival, provides care and nurture and gives a sense of security. These ties, or attachments, influence the way babies and young children feel secure, explore and learn about the world around them, and how they seek help and comfort. The way in which these close emotional ties develop becomes the blueprint for the comfort, care and closeness that babies and young children expect from other important relationships.'

It is important to recognise that this emotional tie will be different in different families and cultures where there are different patterns of care and nurture. Therefore children of differing backgrounds and experiences will have different types of emotional relationships. These relationships will also change over time as the needs of children change. This quote helpfully identifies that early emotional ties support children's development in terms of exploration and learning and also have an impact on future relationships.

In reviewing the literature on attachment relationships beyond the traditional mother-child bond, Howes (1999) states that the key determinants as to whether a child forms a bond with non-maternal caregivers (those who provide care but are not the child's mother) include:

1   whether the caregiver provides both physical and emotional care;

2   whether that person is a consistent presence within the child's social network;

3   whether the caregiver has an emotional investment in the child.

Although this research is based on all those who give care to children beyond mothers, there are some important messages for practitioners who work with young children and babies. Within early years settings, which provide care and education outside the family, this research indicates the need for a consistent early years practitioner who is with the child for stable periods of time. This then creates a predictable pattern in interactions. This Key Person needs provide physical care to the child and invest in the child at an emotional level.

The PSED training materials (Sure Start, 2006) uses three building blocks to explain what is needed to form secure attachments. These are:

1   Feeling secure
2   Separating and exploring
3   Seeking help and comfort

Therefore when babies and young children are more at ease and content, they are likely to feel secure. Once at ease, they feel more able and confident to show interest and explore the world around them. At the same time, they feel safe in the knowledge that there is someone to whom they can turn when comfort and reassurance is needed.

One of the main ways to support the development of secure attachments, emotional warmth and security for young children in early years settings has been to follow the Key Person approach (Elfer, Goldschmied and Selleck, 2003). In this approach, specific practitioners, 'Key Persons', are linked to specific children, 'Key Children.' Elfer et al. describe the Key Person approach as:

'…a way of working in nurseries in which the whole focus and organisation is aimed at enabling and supporting close attachments between individual children and individual staff. The key person approach is an involvement, an individual and reciprocal commitment between a member of staff and a family.'

(p.18)

This is illustrated by the following diagram, which shows the links between the child, the Key Person and the child's parents.

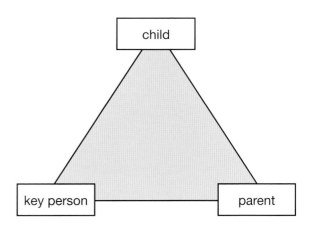

The child is enabled by their close bond with their Key Person to feel secure in the early years setting and therefore enjoys growing independence. The child will be able to separate from their parent and the Key Person, be confident to explore and learn, yet will be aware that they can turn to their Key Person when upset or in need of help or comfort. For this to happen, babies and children need to build a close emotional relationship with one, or perhaps two, key people in their setting. The Key Person should be able to form warm, settled, emotionally close relationships with the children concerned. However, it is important to remember that closeness is not just about seeking help and comfort when distressed or uncomfortable. Moments of enjoyable, shared, special time need to be created so that babies and young children can continue to build and reinforce their special relationship with their Key Person.

What is the Key Person approach in the EYFS?

The EYFS was a central part of the Childcare Act 2006. This legislation focused on improving outcomes for children and reducing inequalities between different groups of children. The Childcare Act 2006 gave legal force to the EYFS in September 2008, when it became mandatory for all schools and early years providers in OFSTED registered settings attended by children aged from birth to the end of the academic year in which the child is five years old.

The EYFS was revised and updated in March 2012 and the revisions were implemented by September 2012. The reformed EYFS were as follows: they intended to reduce paperwork and bureaucracy; further strengthened partnerships between parents and professionals; identified a focus on the three prime areas of learning essential to children's readiness for future learning and healthy development; simplified assessment at the age of five; and provided for early intervention where needed through the introduction of a progress check at the age of two (Overall reforms to the 2012 EYFS Framework, 2012). The revised materials include:

- Updated EYFS Profile guidance
- Remodelled 'Development Matters' material (Early Education, 2012)
- New Statutory Framework for the EYFS (DfE, 2012)
- A summary of the EYFS for parents (Foundation Years, 2012)
- Two-year old progress check guidance (NCB, 2012)

The remodelled Development Matters in the EYFS (Early Education, 2012) replaced the previous Practice Guidance for the EYFS (DCSF, 2008c). The new Statutory Framework for the EYFS (DfE 2012) replaced the previous version (DCSF, 2008a). However, the guidance on implementing the new EYFS states that 'there are NO changes to the principles and commitments in the 2012 EYFS Framework posters and cards' (Foundation Years website, 2012). The website encourages continued use of the posters and principles into practice cards for reflection.

The Statutory Framework for the EYFS (DfE 2012) specifies the learning and development requirements (the seven areas of learning and development and the educational programmes, the early learning goals and the assessment arrangements) and the safeguarding and welfare requirements (steps providers must take to keep children safe and promote their welfare). These requirements are given legal force by an order made under Section 39 (1) of the Childcare Act 2006.

Within the learning and development requirements, the Statutory Framework for the EYFS (DfE 2012) makes a clear requirement in terms of the role of the Key Person:

'Each child must be assigned a key person. Providers must inform parents and/or carers of the name of the key person, and explain their role, when a child starts attending a setting. The key person must help ensure that every child's learning and care is tailored to meet their individual needs. The key person must seek to engage and support parents and/or carers in guiding their child's development at home. They should also help families engage with more specialist support if appropriate.' (p.7, DfE 2012)

This is a stronger and more detailed statement than in the earlier version of the EYFS (DCSF, 2008). Within this requirement, the Statutory Framework highlights the practitioner of the role of the Key Person in terms of relationships with the child and parent/carer rather than being a paperwork-led or administrative role.

Within the safeguarding and welfare requirements, the Statutory Framework for the EYFS (DfE, 2012) states:

'Each child must be assigned a key person. Their role is to help ensure that every child's care is tailored to meet their individual needs, to help the child become familiar with the setting, offer a settled relationship for the child and build a relationship with the parents.' (p.18, DfE, 2012)

In comparison to the learning and development requirement, the safeguarding and welfare requirement highlights the Key Person's role as valuable to individualise the child's experiences, support the child in settling into the setting and building close relationships with the parents.

The Development Matters in the EYFS is non-statutory guidance material intended to support practitioners in implementing the statutory requirements of the EYFS. Within this guidance, the Key Person is included under the practice within the theme 'Positive relationships.' It states that 'Positive relationships are...built on key person relationships in early years settings.' This suggests a continued emphasis on the central role the Key Person plays in babies and young children's lives.

The Development Matters in the EYFS gives guidance for each area of learning and development. Within the prime area of Personal, Social and Emotional Development (PSED), there are a number of statements that relate to the role of the Key Person across all three aspects: Making Relationships, Self-confidence and self-awareness, and Managing feelings and behaviour. These include:

'Make sure babies have their own special person in the setting, who knows them really well and understands their wants and needs.'
(Birth to 11 months/8 – 20 months, PSED: Making Relationships)

'Ensure that the key person or buddy is available to greet a young baby at the beginning of the session, and to hand them over to parents at the end of the session, so the young baby is supported and communication with parents is maintained. '
(Birth to 11 months/8 – 20 months, PSED: Making Relationships)

'Make sure the key person stays close by and provides a secure presence and a refuge at times a child may be feeling anxious.'
(8 – 20 months, PSED: Managing feelings and behaviour)

'Make sure the child can explore from the secure, close-by presence of their key person.'
(16 – 26 months, PSED: Self-confidence and self-awareness)

'Make time for children to be with their key person, individually and in their key group.'
(22 – 36 months, PSED: Making Relationships)

'Ensure that key practitioners offer extra support to children in new situations.'
(22 – 36 months/30 – 50 months, PSED: Self-confidence and self-awareness)

'Ensure children have opportunities to relate to their key person, individually and in small groups.'
(40 – 60 months, PSED: Making Relationships)

While these statements are all within PSED, they demonstrate the need for the Key Person throughout the age range, from birth to the end of the academic year the child is five and that this is central part of how practitioners can promote children's Personal, Social and Emotional Development. In Chapter 4 there is further discussion about how the Key Person can support a child learning EAL in their PSED.

On the reverse of the Principles into Practice card (DCSF, 200d) is the Key Person commitment:

'A key person has special responsibilities for working with a small number of children, giving them the reassurance to feel safe and cared for and building relationships with their parents.'

This emphasises that the role of the Key Person is to work with a number of children and their parents. The use of the word 'small' confirms that the Key Person should have a limited number of children and parents to work with effectively. The commitment also highlights the responsibilities of the Key Person as someone who:

- gives reassurance and comfort to their Key Children;
- enables their Key Children to feel emotionally safe in their environment;
- supports the personal care needs of their Key Children, e.g. toileting, eating, sleeping;
- builds relationships with their Key Children's parents.

The Commitment Card 2.4: Key Person (DCSF, 2008e) expands further on the commitment of Key Persons in terms of shared care, secure attachment and independence. The back of the card:

- provides examples of effective practice from across the age range;
- recognises common challenges and dilemmas that may result from the Key Person approach;
- suggests ideas for reflecting on practice.

The Foundation Years website notes an expectation that many providers will have a Key Person system in place, but suggests using the Commitment Card 2.4 Key Person to reflect on the effectiveness of the Key Person system and how well this works for children and families. The commitment from the card, the details on how to promote secure attachment, and the challenges and dilemmas are highlighted:

- 'A key person helps the baby or child to become familiar with the setting and to feel confident and safe within it.
- A key person develops a genuine bond with children and offers a settled, close relationship.
- When children feel happy and secure in this way they are confident to explore and to try out new things.
- Even when children are older and can hold special people in mind for longer there is still a need for them to have a key person to depend on in the setting, such as their teacher or a teaching assistant.' (Foundation Years website, 2012)

This reinforces the messages within the Statutory Framework for the EYFS (DfE, 2012) and the Development Matters guidance (Early Education, 2012). These are the importance of the key person approach across the age range from birth to the academic year when the child is five with a particular focus on induction and transition to help a child settle and feel confident in their setting. This has particular relevance to children learning English as an Additional Language, who are likely to find it difficult to settle into new rooms and settings.

The challenges and dilemmas are:

- Reassuring others that children will not become too dependent on a Key Person or find it difficult to adjust to being a member of a group.

- Meeting the children's needs for a Key Person while being concerned for staff who may feel over-attached to a child.

- Reassuring parents who may be concerned that children may become more attached to staff than to them.

- Supporting children's transitions within and beyond a setting, particularly as children reach four or five years of age.

The high number of references to and discussion of the Key Person role within the reformed EYFS (DfE 2012) show this to be a central part of the approach to early years care and education in England. These references have continued from the previous version of the EYFS (DCSF 2008a) showing a continuation of a belief in the centrality and importance of the Key Person role.

How can the Key Person approach be used to support children learning EAL?

Children learning EAL have a strong need for a warm relationship that helps them feel cared for and safe, as described in the EYFS. Attending a setting where the child cannot fully understand and speak the language is a stressful experience for both the child and the parents. Therefore both the child and the parent need to have someone clearly identified who they can turn to and rely on, ask questions of and be comfortable with. The Key Person approach is a central part of effectively supporting children learning English as an Additional Language.

Does the Key Person have to speak to same language as their Key Children?

This important question requires some important information gathering first. This includes knowing both:

- the languages the staff speak and understand;

- the languages the child speaks and understands.

It is helpful to have language maps for the staff and the children to help understand the full picture of the languages spoken and understood in the setting. (Examples of language maps are shown in Chapter 2).

If there are staff who work in the setting who speak the same language as the child and parents then this is an important consideration when matching children to a possible Key Person. However, there are many other factors to take into account including:

- the attendance patterns of the child and the working patterns of the staff member;

- who the child is drawn to and bonds with in the setting;

- the personalities and mix of the other children in the Key Person's group.

It is important to not make assumptions and check whether the Key Person does speak the same language/dialect as the child. This is an important part of the induction process and can be done by completing a language map as discussed in Chapter 2.

What can the Key Person do if s/he doesn't speak the same language as the child learning EAL?

1 Identify the key words needed to help support the child to settle in, learn and develop in the setting. Once these key words have been identified, find ways of learning how to say and write them in the child's home language e.g. through translation options on the computer, by asking the parent for key words or by asking other parents or community members.

2 Once the key words have been identified and translated into the child's home language, these need to be used on a regular basis by the Key Person with the child and with others. This helps with communication, but also crucially shows a value and respect for the child's home language. This is an important part of building a positive relationship with the child.

3 The Key Person needs to remember the large percentage of communication that is non-verbal. Mehrabian (1972) is cited as stating that 55% of communication is body language, 38% is the tone of voice, and 7% is the actual words spoken. While this cannot be generalised to all contexts, the main message is that much of a person's communication is shared through body language and tone. Therefore for the Key Person needs to ensure to use his/her body language and tone optimally to build a relationship with the Key Child.

4 The Key Person needs to spend a short amount of time positively with the Key Child daily. This can be by playing with or alongside the child, imitating and reflecting their play and interests. With younger children and babies, this individual time can be spent through care routines such as nappy changing and meal times as well as play. It can be challenging to spend time with a child who you don't share a language with, and therefore it is even more important to communicate your care, interest and attention non-verbally.

5 The Key Person needs to learn to recognise the child's cues in terms of how the child feels. This includes signals for a chance to relax away from the language demands of the environment, signs of frustration or upset alongside cues that indicate the child wants to play or be with you.

6 The Key Person is likely to benefit from using visual clues to support communication with the child. This can be in the form of real objects e.g. a coat to indicate that it is time to go outside or photographs to help the child anticipate what comes next. It is important to recognise the child's stage of development in using these cues to support communication.

7 It is vital that the Key Person learns as much as s/he can about the child. This can be supported by a home visit alongside a child and family record as suggested in Chapter 2. It is important to know what the child likes and is interested in, alongside things that may scare or upset them.

8 Once the Key Person had identified what the child likes and enjoys, it is important to build these interests into visible, concrete experiences that the child can share with others. For example, if a child loves bubbles, then putting bubbles in the water tray may be a great way to help them play confidently with the Key Person and with others.

9 The Key Person plays a central role in helping the child build relationships with other children. This includes relations with children who speak the same language as the child, and also with others. This is aided by simple name games to help children know each others' names, and by giving older children a buddy or responsibilities the children carry out in pairs.

10 Role-play is often a form of play that children enjoy, and it is important that this incorporates objects and items that the child recognises from their own experiences. It can be helpful to visit local community shops where the child may go and have items from there, alongside items from the larger supermarkets.

11 The Key Person needs to build relationships with the child's parents.

How can a Key Person build relationships with the parents of children learning EAL who may not speak much English?

The Key Person needs to build relationships with the parents of children learning English as an Additional Language is in the same way as they do for all parents. It is important to build strong foundations for the relationship at the beginning of the child's time in the setting and this needs to be constantly re-visited and developed.

1   Whenever the child and parent come to the setting, ensure that the parent is greeted alongside the child. This means asking what the parent would like to be called and sharing your own name.

2   As a Key Person it is important to treat the parent as a person in their own right, asking how they are and making good use of verbal and non-verbal communication. Just remember, a smile goes a long way!

3   The Key Person and parent both have one main shared interest: the child. Share the child's successes and experiences at the setting through photographs, videos and things the child has created. This reduces the need for the reliance on words alone.

4   Check out the words you have found to use with the child with the parents. This gives the parent the chance to be an expert and support you, rather than always having to rely on you. This helps create an equal and balanced partnership.

5   Be interested in the parent and family and see the parent as a partner in the child's learning and development.

6   If a more detailed or private conversation is needed, prepare for this in advance by booking a translator or preparing key words, materials and objects to help communicate your message. It is important to book a private room or space. It can be helpful to ask the parent if they want to bring a friend with them to help, but be aware of the sensitivity of the information you are sharing and that this may place the other person in an awkward or uncomfortable position.

7   Be sensitive to the needs of the parent and the child.

Reflecting on the Key Person approach in supporting children learning EAL

Think of the children in the setting who are learning EAL:

■   Why is the named Key Person working with each of these children? What is the thinking behind the allocation? Have the child's languages been taken into accounts?

■   How and when is each Key Person building their relationship with each child learning EAL?

■   How is the Key Person supporting each child learning EAL to build relationships with other children and adults?

■   How is the Key Person recognising and valuing each child's home language?

■   How is the Key Person recognising and valuing each child's culture and home life?

■   How does the Key Person build relationships with the parents and family of each Key Child learning EAL?

The environment for supporting children learning EAL

This chapter examines how the environment can be used to support practice with children learning English as an Additional Language. It looks at the indoor, outdoor and emotional environments. It ends with a reflection tool to use to think about how the environment supports children learning EAL.

The learning environment

The revised EYFS maintained the four themes of the preceding version of the EYFS (DCSF, 2007); a Unique Child, Positive Relationships, Enabling Environments and Learning and Development. The principle of Enabling Environments is:

■ children learn and develop well in Enabling Environments, in which their experiences respond to their individual needs and there is a strong partnership between practitioners and parents and/or carers.

The commitment detailed on the Commitment card; 3.3 The Learning Environment (DCSF, 2008f) is: 'A rich, varied environment supports children's learning and development. It gives them the confidence to explore and learn in secure and safe, yet challenging, indoor and outdoor spaces.' The Principles into Practice card also identifies three important aspects of the learning environment: indoor, outdoor and emotional environment.

The indoor learning environment

The Principle into Practice card on the Learning Environment identifies that the indoor space in an early setting needs to be safe and secure. Many children spend long hours at their early years setting and so it is important that the setting is homely and has different spaces for children to be quiet, to be noisy, to eat and to sleep. The indoor environment should contain resources that are appropriate, well maintained and accessible for all children. It highlights the importance of having planned but flexible spaces indoors to respond to children's changing interests and needs as there is a need for children to have comfort and familiarity but also novelty to stimulate learning at times.

In addition, the Effective Practice article on the Learning Environment (DCSF, 2008g) highlights the following:

■ The space needs to be appropriate for the age and development of all the children using it.

■ The space needs to be appropriately heated and aired and free from hazards.

■ The areas and resources, both natural and manufactured, should be well organised and stimulate all the senses.

■ Both new and familiar materials should be used alongside open-ended resources.

■ There should be opportunities for a range of activities such as soft play, paint mixing, growing plants, mark-making, looking at books, reading stories, or exploring the properties of materials such as clay, sand or water.

■ The indoor environment needs to change and respond to babies' and young children's changing interests and so should be dynamic not static.

Developing the indoor environment for children learning EAL

The Primary National Strategies (2007) guidance for supporting children learning EAL recommends that the learning environment should be organised so that children learning EAL have opportunities to make independent choices. This means that the resources need to be well organised, accessible and labelled pictorially with photographs or with an image of the real object. This allows practitioners to observe what those children learning EAL are interested in and what they are motivated to play with. This relates to discussion of the characteristics of effective learning (see Chapter 7) and allows practitioners to develop the home language or English to support in these activities.

The Primary National Strategies guidance also recommends that the learning environment includes play and learning resources that positively reflect the children's cultural and linguistic identity and experiences. This can be in relation to books and posters reflecting the identity of the children who attend the setting. The easiest way to do this is to use photographs of the children (with parental permission) who attend the setting. Role-play equipment should reflect children's lives and include community language newspapers and food packaging, and display a variety of scripts to support language awareness. Items that reflect children's lives are best gathered from the families that attend the setting and can include shampoo bottles, handbags, keys, scarves, shoes and mobile telephones.

The outdoor learning environment

The Commitment card on the Learning Environment (DCSF, 2008f) identifies that the outdoor environment has a positive impact on children's sense of well-being and helps in all aspects of children's development. It gives children an opportunity for first-hand experiences linked to Understanding of the World as an area of learning as it gives children contact with the weather and natural world. It can also support Physical Development because it allows children space to be physically active and energetic. It recommends that children have daily access to the outdoor environment.

Many of the issues stated for the indoor environment in the Effective Practice article on the Learning Environment (DCSF, 2008g) are also relevant for the outdoor environment: the space used should be appropriate for the age and development of the children; it should be well organised, contain natural and manufactured resources; it should have opportunities for a range of activities; and should change in response to children's interests. In addition, the article highlights the importance of the outdoor environment giving opportunities for risk taking and learning about keeping safe.

The article identifies that outdoor environments should offer a variety of surfaces and levels, places to sit or lie, to climb or swing and to make big movements such as spinning, dancing, jumping and running. There should also be opportunities to dig, climb, swing and control wheeled toys. Children should be able to touch and feel a variety of textures and to move, stretch and crawl. They may like to make marks, to cut and join materials together or to shape and construct materials. Importantly, they also need to be able to rest and take a break when needed.

Learning through Landscapes Early Years: Visions and Values for Outdoor Play adds that:

'The outdoor space and curriculum must harness the special nature of the outdoors, to offer children what the indoors cannot. This should be the focus for outdoor provision, complementing and extending provision indoors.'

This emphasises that the outdoor learning environment should not simply replicate what is on offer in the indoor environment but rather, the outdoor learning environment should complement and extend it. This is because in the outdoors, children can have greater freedom to explore physical space and are more likely to have greater room and permission to be active, messy, noisy and work on a larger scale.

In addition, children may feel less-controlled by adults in the outdoor learning environment. However, it is important to strike a balance here sometimes practitioners can perceive that the outdoor environment is one they should not intervene in and as a result they may interact with children less.

Developing the outdoor environment for children learning EAL

The Primary National Strategies (2007) guidance on supporting children learning EAL identifies opportunities to play outside as particularly beneficial as most children tend to be less inhibited in their language use in an outdoor environment. Practitioner observations have shown that children commonly make at least five times as many utterances outdoors as they do inside.

The Principles into Practice Card highlights the challenge of finding ways to promote the value and importance of the outdoor environment to all those involved in the setting; including practitioners and parents. This is of importance to parents of children learning EAL where the value of outdoor learning must be clear to all parents. This may be best done through visual representation, such as photographs, rather than relying on words alone. There can be concern from all parents that their child will get cold or ill in the outdoor environment. However, photographs showing children's enjoyment and all that they can learn outside can help share the message that outdoor play is important.

The emotional learning environment

The Commitment Card on the Learning Environment (DCSF, 2008f) explains the emotional environment as one that is created by the values and attitudes of the adults in the early years setting. A warm and accepting emotional environment is needed, where practitioners empathise with children and accept expression of a range of emotions. The Commitment Card on the Learning Environment highlights the importance of valuing children's efforts, not just the outcomes. The emotional environment is intangible, but has an important impact on the children and practitioners.

Developing the emotional environment for children learning EAL

The concept of accepting everyone is important for all children and has relevance for children learning EAL as their language development can be viewed either as an asset or as a burden. The Primary National Strategies (2007) guidance on supporting children learning EAL highlights the fact that 'Bilingualism is an asset, and the first language has a continuing and significant role in identity, learning and the acquisition of additional languages.'

Whilst this statement is helpful in terms of giving knowledge to practitioners, it is important that it becomes a core value for practitioners supporting children learning EAL. The guidance goes on to encourage practitioners to examine attitudes and feelings towards children learning EAL. The attitude of practitioners can be supported by gaining knowledge about language development and bilingual language development.

It is also important not to view children learning EAL as a homogenous group; their needs and interests will be individual. As with Special Educational Needs, learning EAL is just part of the picture of the child, but is not the whole child and should not be seen as their defining feature. For practitioners it is vital that they get to know each child as an individual, with their own needs, interests, thoughts and feelings. This includes having a good understanding of the background of the child (see Chapter 2 for a suggested child and family record and language map). It is vital that the children's first names and their family names are correctly spelled and pronounced as this is an intrinsic part of a child's identity. Misspellings or a lack of effort to pronounce names correctly indicates a lack of respect and value.

The Primary National Strategies guidance encourages 'buddies': that if another child speaks the same language, this child can act as a 'buddy' to a new child. It is important that children should be helped as soon as possible to understand that they are learning to speak more than one language and that those languages have names. This is an important part of their identity. The Key Person could be the practitioner who speaks the same language as the child, but this is not the only option (see Chapter 8 about the Key Person role in supporting children learning EAL).

Practitioners using children's home language with children and babies shows to the children that home languages are valued. Babies may be comforted, particularly at rest or sleep times, by songs or stories recorded in their home language by their main carer. Children may find it helpful to be able to tune in to their home language at other times during a long day of unfamiliar speech sounds in English. This gives a welcome respite from the challenge of the day as it brings familiarity and comfort. Children sharing the same first language should be facilitated to play together sensitively as this again shows a value for home language.

Reflecting on developing an Enabling Environment for children Learning EAL

- How are linguistic and cultural diversity visibly celebrated in this setting?

- How is cultural and religious information recorded at admission, including customs, diet, festivals, worship, etc.?

- How does the setting find out about the languages, culture and circumstances of the children learning EAL at the setting?

- How does the setting enable children learning EAL to access routines, activities and equipment?

- How does the setting develop a common understanding about EAL development with partner agencies, particularly health, including speech and language therapists and health visitors and parents?

How to identify and support EAL learners with Special Educational needs

This chapter considers how to identify when children learning EAL have Special Educational Needs. This chapter begins by explaining what Special Educational Needs are, the guidance for supporting children with SEN and ways to identify when children learning EAL have SEN.

What are Special Educational Needs?

The term 'Special Educational Needs' was a legally defined under the 1996 Education Act. Children have Special Educational Needs if they have learning difficulties or disabilities that make it harder for them to learn or access education than most children of the same age. Children have a learning difficulty if they have significantly greater difficulty in learning than the majority of children of the same age or have a disability which prevents or hinders them from making use of educational facilities of a kind generally provided for children of the same age.

Children with SEN need extra help, or help that is different to that given to other children of the same age. This is sometimes called 'special educational provision.' Special educational provision is educational provision that is additional or otherwise different from the provision made generally for children of their age in mainstream schools. This can include using variety of different ways of teaching or extra adult providing some help in a small group perhaps or use of particular special equipment and resources.

While the indicative draft of the (0–25) SEN Code of Practice (DfE, 2013) identifies that about 75% of children with a disability have a special educational need. It is important to remember that the disability and SEN are separate and do not always occur together in children. The Equalities Act (2010) defines disability as:

'A person has a disability for the purposes of this Act if they have a physical or mental impairment which has a substantial and long-term adverse effect on their ability to carry out normal day-to-day activities.'

Many children will have SEN of some kind at some time during their education. Help will usually be provided in their ordinary, mainstream early education setting or school, and sometimes this will be with the help of outside specialists. A few children will need help some of the time or all of the time in their setting. There are four categories of special educational need, which are:

1   communication and interaction (Communication and Language);

2   cognition and learning (Thinking);

3   emotional, social and behavioural development (Personal, Social and Emotional Development);

4   sensory and/or physical development (Physical Development).

Children can have difficulties in one or more areas of those listed above. These can be seen to be linked to the Early Support Developmental journals that focus on the prime areas and thinking. These materials can be found on the National Children's Bureau (NCB) website (www.ncb.org.uk/earlysupport).

The SEN Code of Practice (2001)

The SEN Code of Practice 2001 (due to be revised in 2014) gives practical guidance on how to identify and assess children with Special Educational Needs. All early education settings, state schools, local authorities, health and social services must take account of the current SEN Code of Practice when they are dealing with children who have Special Educational Needs. This means that early education settings, schools, local authorities and health and social services should always consider the Code when they decide how they will help children with Special Educational Needs.

The 2001 SEN Code of Practice includes statutory (what must be done) and non-statutory requirements (what should be done) for teaching practitioner when assessing and making provision for children and young people's SEN. The SEN Code of Practice suggests that a graduated approach is best, as it recognises that children learn in different ways and can have different levels of SEN. So increasingly, step by step, specialist expertise can be brought in to help the setting or school with the difficulties that a child may have.

The indicative Draft: The (0-25) Special Educational Needs Code of Practice (DfE, 2013) identifies a number of principles that underpin all work with children and young people. These include:

- Early identification of needs.
- High expectations and aspirations for what children and young people with SEN and disabilities can achieve.
- Focus on the outcomes that children and young people and their families want to achieve.
- The views and participation of children and their parent/carer and young people are central.
- Choice and control for young people and parents over the support they/ their children receive.
- Education, health and social care partners collaborate for coordinated and tailored support.
- Clarity of roles and responsibilities is needed.
- High-quality provision to meet the needs of most children and young people, alongside rights for those with EHC plans to say where they wish to be educated.
- The skills, knowledge and attitude of those working with children and young people are central to achieving excellent outcomes.

These principles highlight the importance of early intervention, and this is particularly important when working with children learning English as an Additional Language where Special Educational Needs can be seen to be an EAL issue. These principles also indicate the need for every stage of assessing, identifying and supporting children with SEN to be family and child-centred.

A child with SEN may have an Individual Education Plan (IEP) play plan or access some additional support, which may be detailed in a Provision Plan. This needs to detail:

- what help is being given

- how often the child will receive the help
- who will provide the help
- what the targets for the child are
- how and when the child's progress will be checked.

If the child does not make enough progress, the Special Educational Needs Coordinator (SENCO) will then talk to the parents and family of the child to seek advice from other people outside the early years setting. This may include external agencies such as specialist teachers, educational psychologists, speech and language therapists or other health professionals. This kind of help then moves the child to Early Years Action Plus in an early years setting or School Action Plus in a school. However, this guidance is being revised and the new SEN Code of Practice may use different terms of reference in the near future.

Can a child have both Special Educational Needs and English as an Additional Language?

It was not until the Education Act of 1981 (Department of Education and Science) that schools and settings were required by law to distinguish between having Special Educational Needs and learning English as an Additional Language. Practitioners are told not to assume that a lack of English language is linked to a learning problem and low intelligence.

'A child is not to be taken as having a learning difficulty solely because the language (or form of language) in which he is, or will be, taught is different from a language (or form of language) which has at any time been spoken at home.'

(Hall et al., 1995)

Here a distinction is made between children who have learning difficulties because of the language in which s/he is taught, and a child with Special Educational Needs. Nevertheless, it is essential that support is given to children to with EAL to ensure they are given full access to the curriculum during the time they are acquiring an additional language which is matched to their cognitive ability.

It is now recognised that that children do not have learning difficulties just because their first language is not English. However, it is important to recognise that some children with English as an Additional Language may have learning difficulties. Therefore the following three groups of children exist:

Children with English as an Additional Language	Children with Special Educational Needs	Children with English as an Additional Language and Special Educational Needs

However, misidentification can occur or practitioners can fail to identify children. This means that a child with EAL who does not have Special Educational Needs could be falsely identified as having SEN (false positive) and could therefore be mislabelled and subsequently taught in certain ways or using certain resources that are unsuitable. Alternatively, a child learning EAL that actually does have SEN could fail to be recognised as having Special Educational Needs (false negative) and could therefore miss out on the right help and support, which may lead to difficulties becoming even more challenging to support at a later stage. Unfortunately, there is no single assessment that is reliable enough to establish whether a bilingual child has learning difficulties or not so it remains a challenging area.

What do you do if we think a child with English as an Additional Language has Special Educational Needs?

Ideally the child's competency in their home language use should be assessed first. This can be achieved by:

■ talking to parents about how effective they are at communicating at home;

■ closely observing the child within the first few months.

This will enable the practitioner to understand whether the child has a learning difficulty or whether their only difficulty is not being able to speak English. However, this can be a difficult and lengthy task, as there are complexities in separating language from learning and the process can take time.

It is important to ensure all relevant information has been collated from the parents and the setting or school. This includes:

■ a language profile (see Chapter 2);

■ short and long observations focused on the child's communication and language (with a consideration of the child's ability in the three aspects of Communication and Language (CL); speaking, listening and understanding);

■ observations of the child in other areas of learning and development;

■ the child's Learning Journey (containing formative assessments);

■ transition documents (summative assessments collected at regular points in time);

■ time and event samples to give an understanding of the child in a variety of situations.

In addition, video footage from the child in the home environment, with the support of someone who can translate the child's spoken word, is helpful. This information is then used to compare the child with typical development. This may be through using:

■ Development Matters (Early Education, 2012) non-statutory guidance for the Early Years Foundation Stage;

■ Early Years Foundation Stage Profile (depending on the child's age);

■ Language assessment tools such as Wellcomm Speech and Language Assessment toolkit for the Early Years.

This will identify the child's areas of strength and areas for development. Sometimes it can be helpful to undertake observations and assessments alongside the parent, either at home or in the setting, as a child's shyness or reticence can mask their abilities. This can involve asking the parent to make certain requests of their child in home language to assess the child's understanding. This can be helpful both to gain a full assessment of the child's abilities and skills but also to help illustrate the nature of any concerns to the parents/family to enable an open discussion.

The *Every Child a Talker* Guidance (DCSF, 2008h) recommends that practitioners also take other factors of concern into account, such as the length of time the child has been in the setting and other medical or health issues, such as a hearing difficulty or middle ear infection. It can also be helpful to have an overview of the child's place in the family and how they manage at home.

It is essential that practitioners are proactive at an early stage and deal with any concerns they have that a child may have SEN, and that they do not simply assume that the child just needs more time to 'settle in'. Therefore it is important that practitioners monitor and review a child learning EAL, in the same way as would be done with a child who is considered to have possible SEN.

When should Special Educational Needs be identified for a child learning EAL?

Between the ages of birth to two

Many complex needs, developmental and sensory, are identified at birth. Early health assessments, such as the hearing screening test, used to check the hearing of all new-born babies, enable the very early identification of some difficulties. These include medical and physical difficulties such as cerebral palsy and sensory impairments with vision and hearing. Health services, such as paediatricians, GPs and other health visitors who work with families, are an important service to both families and early years' practitioners as they can help them understand the child's needs and the support that is needed. This means some children learning EAL may enter the setting with an already identified special educational need or disability.

There are several forms of support and provision for this age group. One example is the Early Support – a programme underpinned by a set of principles that aim to improve the delivery of services for disabled children, young people and their families. It enables services to coordinate their activity better and provide families with a single point of contact and continuity through key working. There is also a range of materials and tools to enable more effective working with children with disabilities and Special Educational Needs on the National Children's Bureau (NCB) website (www.ncb.org.uk/earlysupport).

There may be a Portage home visiting service, Educational psychologists, early years workers or specialist teachers involved. It is important to get information for children learning EAL in the same way as would be done with other children.

At the progress check at two years to three years

The Statutory Framework for the Early Years Foundation Stage (DfE, 2012) identifies that early years practitioners have to review the progress of children between the age of two and three and must provide parents/carers with a written summary of their child's development in the three prime areas of learning and development; Personal, Social, Emotional Development, Communication and Language and Physical Development. This summary provides an opportunity for practitioners to talk in-depth with parents and carers about their child's development and this is the same for children learning EAL. It may also be a good opportunity for practitioners to share concerns about a child's development alongside asking parents for their view on their child's development. This can be a good time to share and discuss observations of the child's skills in both English and in the home language. If these observations differ significantly across home and setting, this may be a good time to suggest the parent and practitioner work with the child together either at home or in the setting. This can involve the parent playing with the child or asking some simple questions and the practitioner observing, or the practitioner playing with the child and the parent observing. The important thing to remember is that everyone is working together for the benefit of the child, to try to identify if there are any concerns that indicate Special Educational Needs.

At the end of the EYFS Profile

In the final year of the Early Years Foundation Stage (EYFS) in which the child turns five years old – and no later than the end of June in that year – the EYFS Profile has to be completed for each child. For many children this will occur when they are in Reception. The EYFS Profile provides a picture of a child's progress against expected levels and should build on on-going observations, all relevant records held by the setting, discussions with parents and carers and any other adults whom can offer a useful contribution.

However, the communication skills of children for whom English is not their home language are not all the same. These children will be at different stages of learning English and have one or more other languages. The Early Years Foundation Stage Handbook 2013 (Standards and Testing Agency (STA), 2012) clearly states:

'Learning English as an additional language is not a special educational need [...] Underpinning the EYFS Profile assessment is the understanding that language is central to our sense of identity and belonging to a community, and that linguistic diversity is a strength that is recognised and valued.'

For this reason, practitioners have work with parents to find out about a child's prior language experience and any education experienced elsewhere and support them in understanding that a child's home language development will help them to learn English.

Practitioners will need to observe the child over time and raise questions with the parents, and/or bilingual support assistants, to be confident about what the child knows and understands. This is another point at which to consider whether a child learning EAL has SEN.

The Early Years Foundation Stage Handbook 2013 (STA, 2012) outlines three aspects specific to the assessment of children for whom English is not their home language:

- development in their home language;
- development across areas of learning, assessed through their home language;
- development of English.

Within the EYFS Profile, the three Early Learning Goals (ELGs) for Communication and Language and the two ELGs for Literacy must be assessed in relation to the child's competency in English. It is vital to remember that the remaining ELGs may be assessed in the context of any language – including the child's home language and English. This includes the three ELGs for Personal, Social and Emotional Development (PSED), the two ELGs for Physical Development (PD), the two ELGs for Mathematics, the three ELGs for Expressive Arts and Design and the two ELGs for Understanding of the World.

When is a child with English as an Additional Language not a concern with regard to Special Educational Needs?

The guidance from Every Child a Talker (DCSF, 2008h) provides some useful guidance on when children with English as an Additional Language may behave or speak in ways that seem unusual:

- Children with English as an Additional Language may speak their home language to staff and other children while they are in the early years setting. This is part of finding out that different languages exist.

- Children learning EAL may mix two languages in one sentence. This is part of the learning process and should decrease over time.

- Children may go through a silent period before they feel confident to use English. This can last up to a couple of months.

- Children may go through a period of not wanting to use their home language. This may be due to the influence of peers, the dominance of the majority culture or a change in the way that the community or family use their home language.

Reflecting on supporting children learning EAL and whether they have Special Educational Needs

- How do you ensure you correctly identify Special Educational Needs in children learning English as an Additional Language?

- Which tools do you use to help you assess and identify SEN in children learning English as an Additional Language?

- How do you involve parents and children in the identification, assessment and support of SEN in children learning English as an Additional Language?

- How do you maintain high expectations and aspirations for what children and young people with SEN and disabilities can achieve including those learning English as an Additional Language?

Challenges and dilemmas

CHAPTER 11

This chapter acknowledges some of the dilemmas and challenges when supporting children learning EAL. Ten challenges are outlined in brief scenarios. Each scenario is followed by a discussion of why this challenge may come about and possible solutions to the challenge. There are other possible approaches, but the ideas presented here give some initial ideas. The challenges are available in Chapter 12 as a photocopiable resource that can be used in training sessions with practitioners to help them reflect on practice.

CHALLENGE 1: It is difficult to support children learning English as an Additional Language (EAL) as their parents only want them to speak English at the early years setting.

Scenario: Jaswinder has recently started attending Jumping Jets nursery and her mum and dad have asked that staff only speak English to her, as they want her to learn English. Jaswinder speaks Punjabi at home with her family and her older brother uses English at home with her sometimes when they are playing. Prior to starting at Jumping Jets she used to stay with her grandmother, who speaks Punjabi. What should the practitioners do?

Questions to consider:

- Can parents ask for English alone to be spoken to their child?

- Does the child need opportunities to speak her own home language in the nursery?

Remember that the Statutory Framework for the Early Years Foundation Stage (DfE, 2012) states:

'For children whose home language is not English, providers must take reasonable steps to provide opportunities for children to develop and use their home language in play and learning, supporting their language development at home. Providers must also ensure that children have sufficient opportunities to learn and reach a good standard in English language during the EYFS.'

Jaswinder is unlikely to settle in the setting if she is only used to adults and children speaking in her home language, Punjabi, at home. It is important to remind parents that speaking a child's home language at the setting (Jumping Jets) helps the child settle and also play, learn and develop. It is also what the government promote through the Statutory Framework.

The setting should have prepared a statement for parents based on the Statutory Framework for the EYFS that they could have discussed during the induction period. This would help parents understand the nursery's policy and that the practitioners at Jumping Jets are helping all of the children to develop in their home language and in English. This message could then be reinforced by gaining information using the child and family record, the language map and asking for key words in Jaswinder's home language, Punjabi. Jumping Jets should adopt this approach to asking for and using key words should continue through Jaswinder's time at Jumping Jets as she builds new concepts in Literacy, Numeracy, Understanding the World and Expressive Arts and Design.

CHALLENGE 2: It is difficult to support children learning English as an Additional Language (EAL) who are become easily unsettled and upset when they start the setting. They take a long time to settle into the early years setting and this upsets other children.

Scenario: Eleni has recently started attending Skipping Cats Pre-school group and every day she when comes in she is very upset. Eleni speaks Greek at home with her mum and dad and has not attended an early years setting before. How should the practitioners at Skipping Cats help Eleni settle into the setting?

- What approaches and techniques are used to help children settle in early years settings?
- How can parents help practitioners in knowing how to settle their child?

Remember what is stated in the Statutory Framework for the EYFS (DfE, 2012) in relation to the Key Person approach:

'Each child must be assigned a key person. Their role is to help ensure that every child's care is tailored to meet their individual needs. To help the child become familiar with the setting, offer a settled relationship for the child and build a relationship with their parents.'

Eleni needs a Key Person to help her become familiar with the setting and to help her settle in. It is important to first of all identify an appropriate Key Person for Eleni. If there is a practitioner in the setting who can speak or understand Greek, this may be an appropriate Key Person for Eleni. However, this is not the only criteria to bear in mind, as it will depend on which members of staff work the same hours that Eleni attends the setting, and who can build a bond with Eleni. So number of Key Children and patterns of attendance, as well as personality need to be considered.

If Eleni's Key Person, Soraya, doesn't speak Greek, it would be helpful if she could learn some key phrases that could help Eleni settle in. Soraya could ask Eleni's parents for these phrases and words and find out how Eleni's parents calm her at home or if they have a special toy that calms her down. If Eleni's parents can't speak English, then an online translator may be helpful and any phrases or terms from this can be checked with Eleni's parents.

It can also be helpful to think about other children in the setting and whether Eleni is familiar with any of these children outside of Skipping Cats. It can be helpful to ask older siblings or friends to come and visit younger children who are upset as they provide a connection to home, however, this does not always work and needs to be used with care and sensitivity to both Eleni and her sibling's preferences.

CHALLENGE 3: It is difficult to support children learning EAL as they don't understand the rules and set a bad example to other children in the early years setting.

Scenario: Angus has been attending the Early Eagles nursery for about three weeks. Initially he was quiet and followed the other children when they were playing. However, now he keeps running around the setting when the children are asked to sit on the carpet for a story or group time. He speaks German at home with his grandparents and speaks a little English with his dad.

Questions to consider:

- When does the child manage to follow the rules of the setting?
- What are the rules he can follow?
- Are the rules of the setting appropriate and shown or explained clearly for children learning EAL?

Remember that behaviour management procedures and policies need to be in place for all children. The Statutory Framework for the EYFS identifies that: 'Providers must have and implement a behaviour management policy, and procedures. A named practitioner should be responsible for behaviour management in every setting.' Many children test the rules and boundaries in an early years setting and it is important to understand why a child may be doing this. In this case, Angus' behaviour may relate to his understanding of the rules (or lack thereof), his motivation to follow the rules or his desire to avoid certain times of the day.

There may be some rules that Angus can follow. It can help to look at both when Angus follows the rule of sitting on the carpet and when he does not. There may be times of the day when Angus is able to follow the rule of sitting down. If Angus is able to sit down for his lunch when he can hear the lunch trolley coming but not for story or group time it may be that Angus does not understand that he needs to sit down for story or group time.

An alternative explanation is that Angus finds sitting and listening in story time and group time difficult, as he does not understand what is being said and gets bored. It is important to observe Angus at different carpet times to see what he does and when he can sit and listen. The response to this challenge depends what the observations show, it may be that the rules need to be supported by photographs, that story time and group time need to be more visual or that Angus needs to have an active role in these story and group times to support his understanding.

Practitioners could also talk with Angus' parents about how he behaves at home. It may helpful to find out if he is able to sit and listen at home. This could be ascertained through discussion of what he does when he is watching television or how he responds to stories told by his parents. It may be that Angus has a hearing difficulty and therefore finds it difficult to sit for long. It could be that he is able to sit and listen to stories read in his home language, German, or where picture books that interest him are used.

CHALLENGE 4: It is difficult to support children learning EAL if the person who brings the child to and from the setting doesn't speak any English either. It is very difficult to get parents to understand what is needed for an early years setting.

Scenario: Luis speaks Spanish at home with his parents. His parents are doctors at the local hospital and work long shifts. Luis is brought to his nursery class by his grandmother Julia. She does not speak any English and the practitioner wants to ask her to bring some more nappies and that Luis needs a warmer coat to play outside. How can Luis's Key Person, Kayleigh, pass the message to Julia?

Questions to consider:

■ What methods of communication do the setting use with parents?

■ Are the methods of communication with parents varied and do all parents respond?

■ How can communication with parents be improved?

Remember that partnership with parents and/or carers is threaded throughout the Statutory Framework for the EYFS showing that it is a priority for practitioners and settings. Information on the Foundation Years website (www.foundationyears.org.uk) highlights that the revised Statutory Framework strengthens partnerships with parents and professionals. The EYFS Principles in Practice Card: Parents as Partners (DfES, 2007) identifies that: 'When parents and practitioners work together in early years settings, the results have a positive impact on children's development and learning.'

There are leaflets on the Foundation Years website that can be given to parents. These leaflets can be adapted on the website and can be translated and modified by any early years settings. However, communicating with parents by leaflet or letter is rarely effective for all parents, including those who have children learning EAL.

The EYFS Principles in Practice Card: Parents as Partners suggests displaying words in home languages used by the children in the setting and inviting parents to contribute. This list may include the Spanish words for 'nappies' and 'coat' to help Kayleigh, Luis' Key Person, ask for these items from Julia. Kayleigh could also use photographs of items and the real item to support her in her communication with Julia, Luis's grandmother – alongside a smile and positive eye contact. It is important to remember how much communication is non-verbal!

The EYFS card also suggests asking parents who are working or very busy what their preferred time and method of contact is. So in this case, Kayleigh could suggest that she contact Luis' parents by telephone or email or by sending a written message through a communication book with Julia. It is helpful to think about these issues in the induction period whilst Luis is settling in to the nursery class.

CHALLENGE 5: It is difficult to support children learning EAL as they only want them to play with other children and cousins who speak the same home language at the early years setting.

Scenario: Mariam comes from a large family and many of her cousins attend the same nursery class as her. Mariam is a little shy and tends to prefer to find her cousin Zainab, who speaks the same home language, Arabic, to play with and sit with at snack time. Zainab is a lively girl and is now beginning to answer when Mariam is asked a question. Mariam loves role-play with the dolls and handbags and pretending to be like her mum.

Questions to consider:

■ What do the observations of the child show about his/her communication and preferences in the setting?

■ What does the child's Learning Journey show as the child's understanding of English and home language?

■ When do parents get an opportunity to discuss their child's understanding of English and home language?

Remember that the Statutory Framework for the Early Years Foundation Stage (DfE, 2012) states:

'For children whose home language is not English, providers must take reasonable steps to provide opportunities for children to develop and use their home language in play and learning, supporting their language development at home. Providers must also ensure that children have sufficient opportunities to learn and reach a good standard in English language during the EYFS.'

It also states that:

'Ongoing assessment (also known as formative assessment) is an integral part of the learning and development process. It involves practitioners observing children to understand their level of achievement, interests and learning styles, and to then shape learning experiences for each child reflecting those observations.'

The Statutory Framework for the EYFS promotes children continuing to use and develop their home language and also English. The first stage is to undertake some observations to see how much Mariam is communicating (including use of non-verbal gestures such as nodding and shaking her head), and then look at how much Arabic she is using and how much English she is using. It could be that Mariam is using more English that the practitioners think! It will also help to talk to Mariam's parents about her use of English and Arabic at home.

If practitioners note that Mariam is not keen to use English in the setting, they could build upon her interests and motivations that relate to her characteristics of effective learning. Mariam seems to enjoy role-play and so it may be helpful for practitioners to use English with her when role-playing; putting the dolls to bed or going shopping. An alternative approach is to see if there are any other children Mariam is beginning to play with, beyond Zainab, and encourage them to play with her.

An additional suggestion is to run some small group or pair activities and experiences in English with Mariam based on her interests. If Mariam has been observed as happy to join in with singing in English, this may be a good place to start. Or Mariam's parents may tell the setting that she enjoys cooking at home and this could be a useful adult-led activity that Mariam could enjoy and talk about in English either during the activity or in recounting the play through a photograph story.

CHALLENGE 6: It is difficult to support children learning EAL as the handover time can become confused in terms of which language is used. It can get uncomfortable not understanding what parents are asking or saying to their children.

Scenario: When Amar is collected from pre-school, his mother speaks to him in Somali. She seems to question him about everything and his Key Person, Justyna, wonders what she is saying to him and what he is saying back! Justyna tends to leave them to get on with their chats.

Questions to consider:

- Should parents feel comfortable to talk to their children in the setting?

- Should parents feel comfortable to talk to their children in their home language in the setting?

- How can parent's use of home language with their children be viewed in different ways?

Remember that the Statutory Framework for the Early Years Foundation Stage (DfE, 2012) states:

'For children whose home language is not English, providers must take reasonable steps to provide opportunities for children to develop and use their home language in play and learning, supporting their language development at home. Providers must also ensure that children have sufficient opportunities to learn and reach a good standard in English language during the EYFS.'

Remember that partnership with parents and/or carers is threaded throughout the Statutory Framework for the EYFS showing that it is a priority for practitioners. Information on the Foundation Years website (www.foundationyears.org.uk) highlights that the revised Statutory Framework strengthens partnerships with parents and professionals.

The EYFS Principles in Practice Card: Parents as Partners (DfES, 2007) identifies that it is important to talk with parents about their child's progress and development, providing appropriate support for those who do not speak or understand English. It also reminds practitioners to find out greetings used in other languages and to make sure that everyone who enters the setting receives a friendly welcome.

For Amar's mum it may help her feel welcome if Justyna greeted her in Somali and found out how she would like to be addressed. It may be helpful to have photographs of what Amar has done during the session or the week to help Amar's mum talk to him about his day. This could be in printed form, on a whiteboard or in a digital photograph frame. This is a good opportunity for Justyna to demonstrate that both she and the setting value Amar's knowledge of Somali. This is done by supporting Amar's conversation with his mum through use of photographs and asking for some key words to help with Justyna's communication with Amar.

It is difficult not be worried or upset when a practitioner can not understand what is being said. This is a good moment to reflect on how children learning EAL feel. It is also worth reflecting on what parents generally talk about with their child at the end of the day. This tends to be talk about the day, catching up in general and maybe requests to hurry! This type of talk can be viewed as an opportunity by Justyna rather than a threat. It may also help if Justyna learns some key words in Somali to help her join in the conversation.

CHALLENGE 7: It is difficult to support children learning EAL as they do not recognise their name on their peg, at self-registration or on their books as they are only used to seeing their name in a different script.

Scenario: Khaled has recently arrived in England. His parents speak and write in Bengali. He is beginning to use horizontal lines in his emergent writing. Rehena, another Key Person in the setting has remarked in passing that this looks like Bengali. Khaled is unable to find his peg for his coat or his place setting for dinner in his Reception class. These are both labelled with his name in English.

Questions to consider:
- Are different forms of writing valued in the early years setting?
- Where can different forms of script and writing be found in the early years setting?
- Are practitioners aware of the written languages the children see in their lives out of the setting?

Remember that the Statutory Framework for the Early Years Foundation Stage (DfE, 2012) states:

'For children whose home language is not English, providers must take reasonable steps to provide opportunities for children to develop and use their home language in play and learning, supporting their language development at home. Providers must also ensure that children have sufficient opportunities to learn and reach a good standard in English language during the EYFS.'

It is important for practitioners to find out the languages spoken at home but also the languages that are read and written in too. It is important for the setting to value and support literacy development in home language as well as in English. There is a potential danger that practitioners may focus on supporting children in Communication and Language and overlook Literacy. While assessment in both Communication and Language and Literacy is in English in the Early Years Foundation Stage profile, it can be helpful to assess if children can read or write in other forms of script as this will help to understand the child's errors in English.

Khaled may have experienced reading and writing in Bengali and may be able to recognise his name in Bengali, although he does not recognise it in English. It may be helpful to Khaled to have his name card written in Bengali on one side and in English on the other. This is helpful at a practical level, if Khaled can recognise his name in Bengali, but also will demonstrate to Khaled's family and other than his home language is valued in both written and spoken form.

Another way of looking at this may be to consider that Khaled may not understand print carries meaning and so can not find his name, or he may be at the early stages of recognising his name but is not confident in his ability yet. Therefore additional visual cues such as using Khaled's photograph may help Khaled to develop recognition of his name, coat peg and place setting.

CHALLENGE 8: It is difficult to support children learning EAL because sometimes they choose not to speak, even to the adults.

Scenario: Jakub started in the pre-school room in The Oak Tree Nursery three months ago. He attends for 15 hours a week and does not speak to any of the adults in the room, including his Key Person Ali. Jakub speaks Lithuanian at home. He is happy to play on his own and follows the routine of snack time and tidy up time. Jakub gets a bit upset and cries when things are a different in the pre-school room. Jakub does not come to any of the adults when he is upset.

Questions to consider:

- What do the observations of the child show about his/her communication in the setting?
- What does the child's Learning Journey show as the child's understanding of English and home language?
- When do parents get an opportunity to discuss their child's understanding of English and home language?
- What does the child like to listen to or join in with?

Remember the Statutory Framework for the EYFS states:

'Ongoing assessment (also known as formative assessment) is an integral part of the learning and development process. It involves practitioners observing children to understand their level of achievement, interests and learning styles, and to then shape learning experiences for each child reflecting those observations.'

This reminds practitioners of the importance of observation and how this can be used to help identify a child's interests and preferences. The first stage is to undertake some observations to see how much Jakub is communicating (including use of non-verbal gestures such as nodding and shaking her head) to either other children or adults and when this happens. It may be that he is communicating with children although not with adults. Sometimes children also communicate in different spaces such as outside or in the bathroom or role-play area or at different times such as when he is singing or looking at books on his own.

If there is any verbal communication, it would be helpful to note the language used. It will also help to talk to Jakub's parents about his communication at home in both Lithuanian and in English. This could be done by using a language map (see Chapter 2).

It will also be helpful if Ali, Jakub's Key Person, learns some key words in Lithuanian and uses them with Jakub and his family. Jakub may also benefit from being encouraged to play with other children, particularly those who speak the same language as him, through Ali playing with him and inviting other children to join. Alternatively Ali could do some small group or pair activities with Jakub and one or two of the children he shows an interest in.

CHALLENGE 9: It is difficult to support children learning EAL as sometimes their parents do not respond to letters about trips or come to parent's meetings.

Scenario: Anders speaks Swedish at home with his mum and dad. His parents are studying at the local university and are very busy. Anders is usually brought to the setting by an older cousin who looks after him during the day.

Questions to consider:

- What methods of communication do the setting use with parents?
- Are the methods of communication with parents varied and do all parents respond?
- How can communication with parents be improved?

Remember that partnership with parents and/ or carers is threaded throughout the Statutory Framework for the EYFS showing that it is a priority for practitioners and settings. Information on the Foundation Years website (www.foundationyears. org.uk) highlights that the revised Statutory Framework strengthens partnerships with parents and professionals. The EYFS Principles in Practice Card: Parents as Partners (DfES, 2007) identifies that 'When parents and practitioners work together in early years settings, the results have a positive impact on children's development and learning.'

There are leaflets on the Foundation Years website that can be given to parents. These leaflets can be adapted on the website and can be translated and modified by any early years settings. However, communicating with parents by leaflet and letter is rarely effective for all parents including those who have children learning EAL.

The card also suggests asking parents who are working or very busy their preferred time and method of contact. In this case Anders' Key Person could offer to contact his parents by telephone, email or by sending a written message through a communication book with Ander's cousin. It is helpful to think about these issues in the induction period whilst Anders is settling in. However, it may be worth trying to ring Ander's parents to see if they would like to come to Parent's Evening at a different time.

Sending photographs of Anders on a trip may help his parents understand what Anders does at nursery. This can be individual photographs or could involve sending home his Learning Journey to look at over the weekend.

CHALLENGE 10: It is difficult to support children learning EAL as they may have Special Educational Needs and these are much more difficult to recognise. How can practitioners tell the difference between difficulties relating to learning EAL and SEN?

Scenario: Tuija has recently started going to a childminder, Tasmin, four times a week. She has been going for about two months. Tuija's home language is Finnish. Tuija is very quiet and does not understand what Tasmin asks her to do. She plays alongside other children and particularly likes sand and water play but does not really talk at the table and does not like the childminder group. She gets upset whenever they go.

Questions to consider

- What of do observations of Tuija in the three prime areas of learning show?
- What do observations of Tuija speaking Finnish show?
- What do Tuija's parents think of her development?

Remember it is now recognised that that children do not have learning difficulties just because their first language is not English. However, it is important to recognise that some children with English as an Additional Language may also have learning difficulties.

Ideally the child's competency in their home language use should be assessed first. This can be achieved by talking to Tuija's parents about how effective she is at communicating at home and observing Tuija at home. This will enable the practitioner to understand whether Tuija has a learning difficulty or whether their only difficulty is not being able to speak English.

It is important to ensure all relevant information has been collated and includes:

- a language profile (see Chapter 2);
- short and long observations focused on the child's communication and language (with a consideration of the child's ability in the three aspects of Communication and Language (CL); speaking, listening and understanding);
- observations of the child in other areas of learning and development;
- the child's Learning Journey (containing formative assessments);
- transition documents (summative assessments collected at regular points in time);
- time and event samples to give an understanding of the child in a variety of situations.

In addition, video footage from the child in the home environment (with the support of someone who can translate the footage) is helpful. This information is then used to compare the child with typical development. This may be through using:

- Development Matters (Early Education, 2012) non-statutory guidance for the Early Years Foundation Stage;
- Early Years Foundation Stage Profile (depending on the child's age);
- Language assessment tools such as Wellcomm Speech and language Assessment toolkit for the Early Years.

This will lead to identification of the child's areas of strength and areas for development.

Sometimes it can be helpful to undertake observations and assessments alongside the parent, either at home or in the setting, as a child's shyness or reticence can mask their abilities. This can involve asking the parent to make certain requests of their child in home language to assess the child's understanding. This can be helpful both to gain a full assessment of the child's abilities and skills but also to help illustrate the nature of any concerns to the parents/family to enable an open discussion. In this case, practitioners also need to take other factors of concern into account such as the length of time Tuija has been in the setting and medical or health issues.

CHAPTER 12

Reflecting on practice

This chapter is intended to give a number of activities which can be undertaken by managers of early years settings with their staff, children and parents in order to evaluate the effectiveness of support for children learning EAL in their setting.

Evaluate your early years setting practice through assessment of practitioners' knowledge of language development and confidence in supporting children learning EAL

This uses an action research approach whereby the manager works with:

- staff, to reflect on their practice;
- parents;
- children.

Use the table below to check practitioner's knowledge of language development.

Knowledge of Communication and Language development	Rate these statements 1-4 1 – no knowledge 4 – very knowledgeable			
I know about the different aspects of Communication and Language in the EYFS				
I know where to find out more about children's development of Communication and Language				
I know about the different age bands in Communication and Language				

Use the table below to check practitioner's confidence in supporting children learning EAL.

Confidence in supporting children learning EAL	Rate these statements 1-4 1 – no confidence 4 – very confident			
I am confident in supporting children learning EAL in the indoor environment				
I am confident in supporting children learning EAL in the outdoor environment				
I am confident about supporting children learning EAL emotionally				

The Development Matters in the EYFS (Early Education, 2012) is a good place to start to support practitioner's knowledge of the three aspects of Communication and Language development, and how children progress typically within the age bands. It can be helpful to ask practitioners to describe what happens at the different age bands in terms of listening and attention, speaking and understanding. A quiz using different statements from the Development Matters can be posted up and practitioners asked to guess which age band these relate to. It is important that practitioners do not try and memorise the statements but have an understanding of approximately when children should start to say their first words, put two words together, have single-channelled attention or can understand simple sentences etc.

Evaluate the practitioners' knowledge of their Key Children learning EAL

- Ask the practitioner to name all their Key Children.

- Ask the practitioner to name three things they know about their Key Children (including religion and cultural heritage if relevant).

- Ask the practitioners to name all the children learning EAL.

- Ask the practitioner to name what other languages the child speaks or hears at home.

- Ask the practitioner to write down the names of the parents of their Key Children.

This set of questions should be used sensitively with practitioners and are helpful prompts to reflect on whether children learning EAL are seen as individuals in the same way as children speaking English as their first language. It is vital to check if practitioners are saying and spelling names correctly.

Evaluate practitioners' knowledge of their Key Children's home languages

- Ask the practitioner to name the languages that are spoken and understood by the parents and/or extended family of the Key Child.

- Ask the practitioner to name which written languages children experience in their homes.

- Ask the practitioner to list any key words or phrases in home language that are used by the Key Child learning EAL.

It also helps identify if practitioners know about the language backgrounds of their Key Child. The child and family record form and language map (see Chapter 2 for some examples of these forms) may be a useful record to update if practitioners lack any information about their Key Children. If the practitioner does not know any key words or phrases, it may be helpful to discuss ways of finding out key words such as using the internet, talking to parents or other family members, or other practitioners who may speak the same home language as the child.

Evaluate practitioners' knowledge of their Key Children's characteristics of effective learning

- Ask practitioners to note down the name of each Key Child's that is learning EAL, and what motivates that child to learn.

- Ask practitioners to note down the preferred companions, activities, experiences and environment of each Key Child learning EAL, i.e. where the child engages and who with.

- Ask when the child engages in critical thinking and makes links between experiences at home and in the setting.

There are a number of questions given in Chapter 7 that can also be used to help practitioners think more deeply about each Key Child's characteristics of effective learning.

Evaluate your practice through assessment of practitioners' knowledge of how to support the children learning EAL in the prime areas of learning

Use the table below to check practitioner's knowledge of how to support children learning EAL in the prime areas of learning.

Confidence in supporting children learning EAL	Rate these statements 1-4 1 – no confidence 4 – very confident			
I am confident in supporting children learning EAL in Personal, Social and Emotional Development (PSED)				
I am confident in supporting children learning EAL in Communication and Language in their home language				
I am confident about supporting children learning EAL in Communication and Language in English				
I am confident about supporting children learning EAL in Physical Development				

Completion of the above table helps judge a practitioner's confidence. It is also helpful to ask them to identify aspects of their practice that they feel are particularly relevant to support in children learning EAL. This can be completed using the following table.

Practice that supports children learning EAL	Example of practice that supports children learning EAL
How I support children learning EAL in Personal, Social and Emotional Development (PSED)	
How I support children learning EAL in Communication and Language in developing their home language	
How I support children learning EAL in Communication and Language in learning English	

There are further questions to support reflective practice in these prime areas of learning and development at the end of Chapter 4.

Evaluate your practice through assessment of practitioners' knowledge of how to support the children learning EAL in the specific areas of learning

Use the table below to check practitioners confidence in supporting children learning EAL in the specific areas of learning.

Confidence in supporting children learning EAL	Rate these statements 1-4 1 – no confidence 4 – very confident				
I am confident in supporting children learning EAL in Literacy					
I am confident in supporting children learning EAL in Mathematics					
I am confident about supporting children learning EAL in Understanding the World					
I am confident about supporting children learning EAL in Expressive Arts and Design					

Completion of the above table not only helps judge a practitioner's confidence but it is also helpful to ask them to identify aspects of their practice that they feel are particularly relevant to support in children learning EAL. This can be completed using the following table.

Practice that supports children learning EAL	Example of practice that supports children learning EAL
How I support children learning EAL in Literacy	
How I support children learning EAL in Mathematics	
How I support children learning EAL in Understanding the World	
How I support children learning EAL in Expressive Arts and Design	

There are further questions to support reflective practice in these specific areas of learning and development at the end of Chapter 5.

Evaluate the practice of the setting by talking to parents of children learning EAL how they feel about the setting

The questions could include:

- Do you and your family feel valued here?

- What do you like best about this setting?

- What would you like to change about the setting?

- What would like us to stop doing at the setting?

- Do you feel your home language is valued here at the setting?

Evaluate the practice and environment of the setting by observing and talking to the children learning EAL who attend the setting

Observe or ask the children:

- Where, in the setting, do they play, which areas do they enjoy using and spend time in?

- Where, in the setting, they not play, which areas do they not enjoy using or spending time in?

This can be done by drawing a floor plan of the setting (include both indoor and outdoor environments) and observing and then recording where the children learning EAL go and enjoy. This can be done on the basis of staff discussion or on observations. These spaces can be recorded with a smiley face or a tick. The spaces where children do not go or where they misbehave or get upset can be recorded with a sad face or a cross. This helps give a pictorial overview of the setting and the spaces that are working for children learning EAL. The spaces with the sad faces or crosses can be discussed by the staff as a team, to consider how these can be improved and developed. Often spaces that work well for children learning EAL work well for everyone!

This can also be done in relation to the running of the setting or routines of the day. Write down what happens at different times of the day on a piece of paper. The starting point should be the time the setting opens and the end point the time when the setting shuts. Review when the children learning EAL are happiest and record this by drawing on a smiley face or a tick. At times when they are sad or anxious or angry draw the relevant face or a cross. This is easiest to do when focusing on one or two children learning EAL at a time. This gives an overview of how the children are feeling as the day progresses and may help create a talking point for staff in terms of how can there be more smiley faces on the timeline of the day. A partially completed example is shown below.

Time	Activity	How child learning EAL feels/ behaves
7.30	Doors open – breakfast available	
8.00	Breakfast ongoing	
8.30		
9.00	Go into our room base	
9.30		
10.00		
10.30		
11.00		
11.30		

References

4children (2012) *Parents' Guide to the EYFS Framework*. Foundation Years website: www.foundationyears.co.uk, accessed 8.10.12.

Ainsworth, M., Blehar, M., Waters, E., and Wall, S., (1978) *Patterns of attachment*. Hillsdale, NJ: Lawrence Erlbaum and Associates.

Baker, C. (1996) *Foundations of Bilingual Education and Bilingualism*. Cleveland: Multilingual Matters.

Baker, C. (2007) *A Parents' and Teachers' Guide to Bilingualism*. MPG Books Ltd

Bowlby, J. (1953) *Child care and the growth of love*. Harmondsworth: Penguin.

Bowlby, J. (1969) *Attachment and loss Volume 1: Attachment*. New York: Basic Books.

Bowlby, J. (1973) *Attachment and loss Volume 2: Separation*. New York: Basic Books.

Bowlby, J. (1980) *Attachment and loss Volume 3: Loss*. New York: Basic Books.

Buckley, B. (2003) *Children's Communication Skills: From Birth to Five*. Oxon: Routledge.

David, T., Gouch, K., Powell, S. and Abbott, L. (2003) *'Birth to Three Matters: A Review of the Literature.'* Research Report Number 444. Nottingham: Queen's Printer.

DCSF (2008a) *Statutory Framework for the Early Years Foundation Stage*. Nottingham: DCSF Publications.

DCSF (2008b) *Effective Practice: Observation, assessment and planning*. Nottingham: DCSF Publications.

DCSF (2008c) *Practice Guidance for the Early Years Foundation Stage*. Nottingham: DCSF Publications.

DCSF (2008d) *Principles into Practice card (EYFS)*. Nottingham: DCSF Publications.

DCSF (2008e) *2.4 Key Person Commitment Card (EYFS)*. Nottingham: DCSF Publications.

DCSF (2008f) *3.1 The Learning Environment Commitment Card (EYFS)*. Nottingham: DCSF Publications.

DCSF (2008g) *Effective Practice: The Learning Environment*. Nottingham: DCSF Publications.

DCSF (2008h) *Every Child a Talker: Guidance for Early Language Lead Practitioners*. Nottingham: DCSF Publications.

DfE (2012) *Statutory Framework for the Early Years Foundation Stage*. DfE website: www.dfe.gov.uk.

DfE (2013) *'The Indicative Draft: The (0-25) Special Educational Needs Code of Practice.'* DfE website: www.dfe.gov.uk.

DfES (2007) *Principles in Practice Card: Parents as Partners (EYFS)*.

Early Education (2012) *Development Matters in the EYFS*. London: Early Education.

Elfer, P., Goldschmied, E. and Selleck, D. (2003) *Key Persons in the Nursery*. Oxon: David Fulton Publishers.

Evangelou, M., Sylva, K., Kyriacou, M., Wild, M. and Glenny, G. (2009) *'Early Years Learning and Development Review.'* Research Report DCSF-RR176. DCSF/University of Oxford.

Foundation Years website (2012) *Parent's Guide to the EYFS*. Foundation Years website: www.foundationyears.org.uk.

Hall, D. (2001) *Assessing the Needs of Bilingual Pupils*. 2nd edition, Oxon: David Fulton Publishers.

Hall, D. Griffiths, D., Haslam, L. and Y. Wilkin (1995) *Assessing the Needs of Bilingual Pupils*. Oxon: David Fulton Publishers.

Harding-Esch, E. and Riley, P. (1986) *The Bilingual Family: A handbook for parents*. Cambridge: Cambridge University Press.

Howes, C. (1999) 'Attachment relationships in the context of multiple carers' in J. Cassidy and P.R. Shaver (eds) *Handbook of Attachment*, New York: The Guildford Press. pp.671-687.

Mehrabian, A. (1972) *Nonverbal Communication*. New Brunswick: Aldine Transaction.

National Children's Bureau (NCB) (2012) *A Know How Guide: The EYFS Progress Check at 2*. National Children's Bureau website: www.ncb.org.uk/ey/peertopeersupport.

Primary National Strategy (2007) *Supporting children learning English as an Additional language*. Nottingham: DCSF Publications.

Smidt, S. (2008) *Supporting Multilingual Learners in the Early Years*. Oxon: Routledge.

Sure Start (2006) *Personal, Social and Emotional Development (PSED) Training materials birth to five*. Sure Start website: www.surestart.gov.uk.

Stewart, N. (2011) *'How children learn: The characteristics of effective learning'*, The British Association for Early Childhood Education.

Standards and Testing Agency (STA) (2012) *Early Years Foundation Stage Handbook 2013*. Department for Education website: www.dfe.gov.uk.

Tickell, C. (2011) *The Early Years Foundation Stage (EYFS) Review: Report on the Evidence*. DfE Publications.

Trevarthen, C. (1988) 'Universal cooperative motives: How infants begin to know language and skills in culture' in G. Jahoda and I.M. Lewis (eds) *Acquiring Culture: Cross-Cultural Studies in Child Development*. New York: Croom Helm. pp.37-90.